bs

29.11.06

The Transfer of Learning

The Transfer
of Learning

Participants' Perspectives of Adult
Education and Training

SARAH LEBERMAN, LEX MCDONALD
AND STEPHANIE DOYLE

GOWER

Published by
Gower Publishing Limited
Gower House
Croft Road
Aldershot
Hampshire
GU11 3HR
England

Gower Publishing Company
Suite 420
101 Cherry Street
Burlington
VT 05401-4405
USA

Sarah Leberman, Lex McDonald and Stephanie Doyle have asserted their moral right under the Copyright, Designs and Patents Act, 1988, to be identified as the authors of this work.

British Library Cataloguing in Publication Data
Leberman, Sarah
    The transfer of learning : participants' perspectives of
    adult education and training
    1. Transfer of training 2. Adult learning 3. Employees -
    Training of
    I. Title II. McDonald, Lex III. Doyle, Stephanie, 1953-
    370.1'523

    ISBN-10: 0 566 08734 0
    ISBN-13: 978-0-566-08734-9

Library of Congress Cataloging-in-Publication Data
Leberman, Sarah.
    The transfer of learning : participants' perspectives of adult education and training / by
    Sarah Leberman, Lex McDonald and Stephanie Doyle.
        p.cm.
    Includes bibliographical references and index.
    ISBN-13: 978-0-566-08734-9 (alk. paper)
    ISBN-10: 0-566-08734-0 (alk. paper)
    1. Transfer of training. 2. Adult learning. 3. Transfer of training--Case studies. 4. Adult
    learning--Case studies. I.
McDonald, Lex. II. Doyle, Stephanie, 1953- III. Title.

    LB1059.L335 2006
    374--dc22

                                                                        2006020640

Printed and bound in Great Britain by TJ International Ltd, Padstow, Cornwall.

Contents

List of Figures

List of Tables

Preface

This book brings together theory, research and our experiences on transfer of learning, which is a term used to refer to how an individual's learning impacts upon later learning. Although interest in transfer is over 100 years old, in more recent times there have been increasing demands for learning to have impact and, today, in education, psychology and management considerable research and theory building has given us more insight into the area. However, as the reader will soon find, transfer is a complex and multifaceted concept and one that has engendered considerable debate and controversy.

The authors are all working in the tertiary setting, but come from very different backgrounds. Although this book is intended for students and their tutors/lecturers in the tertiary setting it will have wide appeal to all people involved in preparing others to use their learning so that it (eventually) impacts on-the-job. Even with basic foundation learning programmes, whether they are academically or vocationally inclined, we would expect novices to be able to project beyond their immediate learning and extend this to future learning. This book then will be useful to all students engaged in learning, their supervisors and the management staff. Although many professional/vocational development staff and trainers are aware of the need to transfer learning, the literature would indicate that few are accomplished in the area of transfer technology and application and we would therefore suggest that this book is particularly important for them. In many respects this book is unique because the case studies have adopted a phenomenological approach, which has emphasised the perceptions of the adult learner, rather than the findings of others about them. This makes it a particularly valuable contribution to the education and training literature.

This book will therefore appeal to readers who share our views on the following:

- Transfer of learning is essentially the crux of all learning.
- The concept of transfer is cross-disciplinary and has applicability in many domains of life.
- Knowledge of transfer is essential for all learners and their educator or supervisors who want to improve and facilitate future learning.
- The translating of this knowledge into skills and practice is best accomplished if undertaken in a strategic manner.
- Transfer of learning is best accomplished when it meets the specific needs of the context and cannot be regarded as a set of standard, procedural guidelines.
- Empowering learners with transfer technology is an important component to ensure independence in learning.

It is the intention of this book that these key ideas be introduced via the literature and our case studies. The phenomenological emphasis highlights these positions and brings the reader to a closer examination of them. The case studies will make many connections of personal relevance to the reader.

There are three main parts to this book. The first part covers the nature of transfer and the issues surrounding it. This is followed by the authors' three case studies and the third section reflects upon these case studies. The literature focus is international, but the case studies relate to research undertaken in New Zealand and in a small Pacific island nation, the Cook Islands. This provides the reader with a range of opportunities to transfer their own experiences to these settings and contexts as well as make comparisons and then create new schemas for future reference.

This book is designed to be read according to your requirements. It does not have to be read from cover to cover, as each chapter stands alone, but at the same time it is integrated to provide a comprehensive overview of the transfer of learning.

Chapter 2 provides an overview of the key concepts, theories and approaches associated with the transfer of learning and is intended to give the reader a conceptual understanding of transfer. The formal disciplines, behavioural, generalisation and cognitive approaches to transfer are discussed in depth, with reference also made to Gestalt theory. Specific work-based approaches to transfer are highlighted, including the transfer matrix, the socio-technical model, workplace learning and the role of culture on transfer. The chapter concludes with a discussion of Haskell's general theory of transfer and with some recent developments in conceptualising transfer.

The key principles and ideas of learning as they relate to transfer are discussed in Chapter 3. The characteristics of adult learners are identified. Then the role of professional development and change theories in terms of their effect on the transfer of learning are examined. This is followed by a review of selected approaches to adult learning including experiential and action learning, situated, collaborative and transformative learning.

Chapters 4, 5 and 6 provide case studies of the transfer of learning within the tertiary context, from a management, cultural and distance learning perspective respectively. Case managers working for a government accident compensation organisation are the focus of Chapter 4. They provide a longitudinal perspective on the transfer of learning from the classroom to the workplace. The role of culture on the transfer of learning is highlighted in Chapter 5, where Cook Islands teachers reflect on their professional development and transfer to the classroom. Chapter 6 presents the views of Bachelor of Business Studies students from the Correspondence School on the transfer of learning. The particular emphasis in this case study is on the integration of living and learning.

The factors which facilitate transfer are highlighted in Chapter 7. Particular attention is paid to the three areas highlighted in the first two chapters – learner characteristics, course design and workplace characteristics. Throughout the chapter links are made back to the case studies to illustrate particular points.

Chapter 8 provides concrete examples of the process of transfer. In this chapter we have attempted to exemplify a key concept that arose from each of the case studies. The aim was to model transfer by us reflecting on the research we had completed and highlighting one particular aspect. The three aspects are – personal and professional development, support and preparation for future transfer. This chapter concludes the book and highlights the key considerations for facilitating transfer, as identified by course participants, in different learning contexts.

For readers who are interested in further research in the area of transfer of learning, the Appendix provides a number of suggestions based on the case study findings.

Sarah Leberman, Lex McDonald and Stephanie Doyle

Acknowledgements

This book has been a long time in the making and it is great to see it finally published. The journey has been a true learning experience.

I would particularly like to thank Brett, for shouldering more than his fair share of being a Dad, looking after Phoebe, spending evenings alone and for always supporting me wholeheartedly in whatever I set out to do. I hope that in some small way this book will prepare educators to the extent that Phoebe may benefit from their knowledge and expertise in years to come as she moves through the education system, and as such gain the enjoyment I have had from being involved in learning for as long as I can remember.

Sarah Leberman

We would like to thank Belinda Cattermole for her tireless editing and at times very insightful suggestions. Liz Jones also offered assistance at an early stage and this was much appreciated. Thank you also to Brigit Eames from the Department of Management, Massey University for all her help in creating some of the figures and tables.

Thank you to Fiona Martin at Gower Publishing who was very helpful in responding to questions readily and in a timely manner. Your efficiency and assistance has made the process a good learning experience.

Thank you also to David Boud, David Walker, Mary Broad, John Newstrom and Farhad Analoui for granting permission to reprint their figures as follows:

Figure 1.1: Model for promoting learning from experience (Boud and Walker, 1990, p.67). Reproduced with permission from the authors. David Boud and David Walker. *Making the most of experience. Studies in Continuing Education*, 12 (2), 61-80.

Figure 2.2: The Transfer Matrix; Nine possible role/time combinations (Broad and Newstrom, 1992, p.52). Reprinted with permission of the authors. Mary L. Broad and John W. Newstrom. *Transfer of Training: Action-Packed Strategies to ensure High Payoff from Training Investments*. 1992. Addison-Wesley Publishing Company.

Figure 2.3: A Taxonomy of the socio-technical model of transfer and types of training situations (Analoui, 1993, p.123). Reprinted with permission of the author. Farhad Analoui. *Training and transfer of learning*. 1993. Avebury Publishing.

Sarah Leberman, Lex McDonald and Stephanie Doyle

1 *Introduction*

This book is about the transfer of learning and how it applies in a number of different contexts. We argue that the transfer of learning is a pervading concept that is intrinsically linked to the way we lead our lives everyday. In a fast paced changing society, it is becoming increasingly important for people to embrace life-long learning and to be able to transfer what they have learned to a myriad of different situations. The case studies presented in this book draw on the authors' research in the areas of management, in-service teacher development and business education. These highlight the issue of transfer from the tertiary learner's perspective, an aspect, which to date, has been neglected in the transfer literature.

This first chapter will consider what transfer of learning is, why it is important, highlight the key elements involved in the transfer process, as well as consider contextual issues.

What is transfer of learning?

What is meant by the transfer of learning? When we talk about the transfer of learning we are interested in the extent to which learning is transferred from one context to another. Transfer of training is often used synonymously with transfer of learning. Within this book transfer of training is considered a subset of transfer of learning.

Transfer of learning has been discussed in a number of different contexts, including education, psychology and management and as such has been defined in a number of ways. Some examples are:

- The effective and continuing application by trainees to their jobs, of knowledge and skills gained in training – both on and off the job (Broad and Newstrom, 1992, p.6).
- Real transfer happens when people carry over something they learned in one context to a 'significantly different' context (Fogarty et al., 1992, p.x).
- Transfer is the application of knowledge learned in one setting or for one purpose to another setting and/or purpose (Gagne et al., 1993, p.235).
- Transfer of learning is a fundamental assumption of educators. We trust that whatever is learned will be retained or remembered over some interval of time and used in appropriate situations (Ripple and Drinkwater, 1982, p. 1947).
- In a sense any learning requires a modicum of transfer. To say that learning has occurred means that the person can display that learning *later* (Perkins and Salomon, 1996a, p.423).

The terms 'training' and 'learning' are often used synonymously, but they can also be taken to mean different things. Training elicits thoughts of working on particular skills and can appear very task-focused, the outcome being, of course, learning. Learning, however, seems to be a much broader term, encompassing not only specific skills, but also socio-cultural, cognitive and behavioural characteristics. Despite the terminology debate, Cormier and Hagman (1987) argue that the term transfer of training equates to the term transfer of learning.

The very concept of transfer has also engendered considerable debate (Mestre, 2005). Some believe it rarely occurs (for example, Detterman, 1993), others deem it to be an unworkable concept (for example, Hammer et al., 2005) and to others it is ubiquitous (for example, Dyson, 1999). However, as Mestre notes, the problem in proving transfer is connected to the narrow and reductionist definition it is given and if a more generalist approach is adopted, and less emphasis given to the stimulus generalisation view, then the identification of transfer would be less problematic. For example, as Bransford and Schwartz (1999) observe, transfer is best defined in terms of preparation for future learning, not in terms of identical elements.

In general terms, transfer of learning occurs when prior-learned knowledge and skills affect the way in which new knowledge and skills are learned and performed. Transfer is deemed to be positive if acquisition and performance are facilitated, and negative if they are impeded (Cormier and Hagman, 1987; Marini and Genereux, 1995). Seen in the specific context of transfer, following an identified period of learning related to an individual's place of work, transfer is the process of applying skills, knowledge and attitudes acquired during a training programme to the work place. Their successful application leads to an improvement in job performance and has a lasting effect. McGeoch and Irion (1952 cited in Cormier and Hagman, 1987, p.xi) suggest that transfer of learning 'is one of the most general phenomena of learning and, by means of its influence, almost all learned behaviour is interrelated in complex ways'.

In the field of psychology there has been an interest in transfer of learning since the beginning of the century. However, it was not until the 1960s and 1970s that the methodology of transfer experiments was used in other areas of human learning. Marini and Genereux (1995) approach transfer of learning from an educational perspective. They suggest that in the past there has been a separation of the transfer process into task, learner and context, rather than taking a holistic approach. They argue that in order to optimise transfer, it is necessary to teach about content/conceptual knowledge, procedural/strategic knowledge and appropriate dispositions.

A differing view of transfer is suggested by Bereiter (1995), who considers transfer to be an ability or as a set of dispositions, not a process, with the potential for transfer lying with the learner, rather than in what has been learned. He argues that teaching should focus on character education, so that learners are able to think about situations rather than try and reproduce their learning. He supports the work of Lave and Wenger (1991) who argue that people learn by entering ongoing 'communities of practice' and gradually work their way into full participation. This of course underscores the importance of the social-cultural context.

Given the above discussion, transfer in the context of this book is regarded as a process, where the learner plays a key role. This transfer process may involve a number of participants, primarily the learner, the educator or facilitator and the colleague or manager, who play different parts in the various phases of the transfer process – before, during and after initial learning.

Why is transfer of learning important?

There is no more important topic in the whole psychology of learning than transfer of learning ... Practically all educational and training programs are built upon the fundamental premise that human beings have the ability to transfer what they have learned from one situation to another ... The basic psychological problem in the transfer of learning pervades the whole psychology of human training ... There is no point to education apart from transfer.

(Desse, 1958, p.213)

There is considerable debate about the nature and occurrence of transfer, as well as an unequivocal awareness of the central importance of transfer. We suggest that there are a number of reasons why this has occurred:

- There is recognition that transfer is a core concept in learning and relates to both process and outcome. It helps us learn by facilitating the storage, processing, remembering, and retrieving of information. Every time learning occurs previous learning is used as a building block. Not only is it the very foundation of all subsequent learning, but it is also important for other cognitive activities such as thinking, reasoning, planning, metacognition, decision-making and problem solving. It is therefore the very essence of understanding, interacting and creating. Furthermore, it is the ultimate aim of teaching and learning. Numerous reports on the state of education (see for example, Bennet, 1993; Bloom, 1987; Gardner, 1991; Hirsch, 1987) have identified transfer of learning as a fundamental issue and, increasingly, its importance in tertiary education courses has been highlighted (see for example, Assiter, 1995; Cargill, 2004; Halpern and Hakel, 2003; Lister, 2003; Thompson et al., 2003).
- In a world in which globalisation, technological advances and increased interdependence are required, there is an increasing acknowledgement that we need information and thinking that will transfer. As Haskell (2001) observes, the Information Age necessitates innovative responses and some (for example, Senge et al., 1994) see the need for organisations to reposition themselves as learning organisations to maintain high quality outcomes. A key prerequisite of this is, of course, transfer of learning. The rapid growth in knowledge, technology and scientific change combined with the frequent job changes of workers will favour those who have a broad-based and transferable set of behaviours and skills. Life-long learning has become a necessity and transfer of learning provides the vehicle for this to occur.
- The trainee and employer want transfer to occur, but there is a clear understanding that education and training is often too theoretical, and consequently there is a failure to integrate the learning and for the training to impact on-the-job (Haskell, 2001). This promotes disillusionment and frustration in trainees and management alike. Attention to the needs of the individual learner and the organisation require balancing, so that the transfer outcomes benefit both and enhance development.
- Improved accountability and evaluation systems have highlighted the importance of return-on-investment and the need to promote education and training programmes that do have impact (Phillips, 1996; Williams et al., 2003). Throughout the world, large amounts of funding are devoted to training and it is suggested that the impact is often minimal (Williams et al., 2003). Indeed, there is little empirical evidence to suggest that training is linked to improved job performance or employee attitude (Faerman and Ban, 1993).

Many educators believe the transfer of learning is the most significant issue for their practice (Bereiter, 1995; Cargill, 2004; Halpern and Hakel, 2003; Thompson et al., 2003). For employers and employees it is an issue of organisational sustainability and personal survival (Bresnen et al., 2003; Broad, 2005; Broad and Newstrom, 1992; Noe and Colquitt, 2002; Thompson et al., 2003). At the adult and tertiary levels of education and training its central importance is now increasingly being related to job proficiency, personal employability and well-being (Berryman, 1993; Bransford and Schwartz, 1999; Lister, 2003; Misko, 1995; Thompson et al., 2003)

Overview of different levels and types of transfer

The levels of transfer are often referred to as positive and negative. In addition, there are both subtle and marked differences in types of transfer. Many of the differences lead to distinctions in how transfer is classified depending on the level of complexity of the transfer.

POSITIVE TRANSFER

When learning in one context improves learning or performance in another context this is called positive transfer. For example, if someone learning a new database package has background knowledge of databases or has used a different database package they are likely to benefit in terms of time taken to learn the new package. Or, for example, the previous experience of learning algebra facilitates learning statistics.

NEGATIVE TRANSFER

Negative transfer occurs when previous learning or experience inhibits or interferes with learning or performance in a new context. For instance, a person for whom schooling was an unpleasant experience may avoid 'classroom' situations. It is common for tourists accustomed to driving on the right hand side of the road to experience difficulty adjusting to driving on the left hand side in New Zealand and Australia. Bransford, Brown and Cocking (2000) suggest that previous experiences or learning can hinder the learning of new concepts. They provide the example of where the prior experience of learning to walk upright, on what appears to be a flat earth, hinders the learning of concepts in physics and astronomy.

SIMPLE VERSUS COMPLEX TRANSFER

Simple transfer happens when little or no effort is required to apply what has been learned in one situation to a new situation. In class, students are taught how to use a spreadsheet to create a budget. Later they need to create a budget for a club trip, and set up a spreadsheet for this. This is an example of simple transfer. However, if the same students were engaged in gathering data for a research project and thought about the ways in which the spreadsheeting program could assist with the data management and analysis, this would be an example of more complex transfer.

NEAR AND FAR TRANSFER

Another distinction used is between near and far transfer. Usually these terms distinguish the closeness or distance between the original learning and the transfer task, for example, learning to shift gears in a truck is an example of near transfer for someone who has already learned to shift gears in a car. Near transfer has also been seen as the transfer of learning within the school context, or between a school task and a very similar task. For example, when students answer similar questions in tests to those they have practised in class. Far transfer is used to refer to the transfer of learning from the school context to a non-school context. For example, skills learned in mathematics such as taking care and checking all alternatives, when used in making investment decisions is an example of far transfer.

AUTOMATIC AND MINDFUL TRANSFER

When an individual responds spontaneously within a transfer situation, which is very similar to the learning situation then this is automatic transfer. For instance, learning to read English in one class, results in the learner automatically reading English language in another context.

Perkins and Salomon (1996b) use the terms low and high road transfer to differentiate the mechanisms of automatic and mindful transfer. Gradually, with time and practice, the automatic transfer effect will extend or 'reach out' over the low road. For example, the school student who is reading and writing in diverse subjects is slowly and gradually gaining expertise in reading English. In contrast, mindful, high road transfer is deliberate and involves conscious thought and intellectual effort, and occurs in situations where there are significant gaps or differences between the original and the transfer situations.

In an education or training course participants learn about a process in a controlled environment. The problems encountered in the educational setting tend to be well defined. In the workplace it may not always be obvious when, or even desirable to use the procedure. For example, there tend to be lengthy delays when a key person is absent, and a substantial backlog of work. The surface question is what could be done to speed up the process, and to automate it as much as possible. However, in real life other problems could arise: the staff member is proud of their existing system; the existing system is not documented; does the operating system used by the company support the software required; what about the compatibility between branches; what about staff training; is there money in the budget and will a transition period be required?

The transfer context

A CONCEPTUAL MODEL

The case studies in this book are based on participant perspectives of transfer in three different contexts – management, in-service teacher development and education. In order to find a conceptual model which encompassed these, we needed to identify the commonalities in the case studies. All involved adult learners who brought a range of experiences, knowledge and skills to the learning environment. Similarly, all were participating in order to enhance the particular situation they were in. We concluded that the key for all our participants was to be able to promote learning from experience and that for the transfer of learning to be maximised a number of important factors needed to be considered. These include: the participants in the process, the different time periods associated with transfer, the socio-cultural environment of both, the workplace and the learning context, as well as programme design.

Boud and Walker (1990) developed a model for promoting learning from experience where the personal foundation of experience and the intent of the experience are important concepts. Both of these were identified as commonalities in our case studies as discussed above. The model is shown in Figure 1.1 (Boud and Walker, 1990) and emphasises the importance of the reflective process in learning from experience to facilitate the transfer of learning to new situations.

The focus in Boud and Walker's model is on the learner and the environment in which the learning takes place, as well as the skill set and preparation the learner brings with them to the learning experience. During the experience the learner will be, either consciously or subconsciously, making links to prior learning within their own lived experience, represented by the central part of the model shown in Figure 1.1. The reflective processes shown on the right hand side of Figure 1.1 represent the time post-experience and are crucial for the transfer of learning to occur in different contexts.

Summary

This chapter has introduced the concept of transfer and identified some of the key issues relating to understanding the process. Transfer is concerned with prior learning affecting new learning and it is introduced here not in an individualistic manner, but as a process that needs to be considered in holistic terms with reference to the learner and environment. However, as indicated, it is complex, multifaceted and at times a confusing process, but one that is important to understand because it is so intimately related to training and education and therefore pivotal in promoting learning. In the fields of education, psychology and management it is recognised as a central concept that facilitates all development and yet many people working in these areas do not adequately understand transfer technology. Furthermore, the global and technological society demands more than ever that a worker has the ability to transfer information, thinking and skills. Both employers and employees expect transfer to occur. The Boud and Walker model introduced in this chapter provides a most appropriate conceptual approach for understanding how we view transfer and for interpreting our case studies. In the following chapter a range of approaches and perspectives on transfer are outlined and provide the reader with a broad base for understanding transfer.

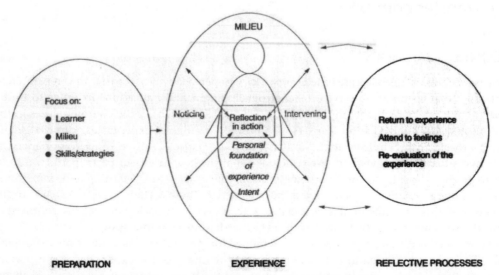

Figure 1.1   Model for promoting learning from experience (Boud and Walker, 1990, p. 67 – reprinted with permission of the authors)

References

Assiter, A. (ed.) (1995).*Transferable Skills in Higher Education,* Kogan Page, London.

Bennet, W. (1993). *The Book of Virtues,* Simon & Schuster, New York.

Bereiter, C. (1995). In *Teaching for Transfer: Fostering Generalization in Learning.*(eds, McKeough, A., Lupart, J. and Marini, A.) Lawrence Erlbaum Associates, Mahwah, NJ, pp. 21–34.

Berryman, S. E. (1993). *Review of Research in Education,* **19,** 343–401.

Bloom, A. (1987). *The Closing of the American Mind,* Simon & Schuster, New York.

Boud, D. and Walker, D. (1990). *Studies in Continuing Education,* **12,** 61–80.

Bransford, J. D., Brown, A. L. and Cocking, R. R. (eds) (2000). *How People Learn: Brain, Mind, Experience and School,* National Academy Press, Washington DC.

Bransford, J. D. and Schwartz, D. L. (1999). *Review of Research in Education,* **24,** 61–100.

Bresnen, M., Edelman, L., Newell, S., Scarborough, H. and Swan, J. (2003). *International Journal of Project Management,* **21,** 157–66.

Broad, M. L. (2005). *Beyond Transfer of Training: Engaging Systems to Improve Performance,* Pfeiffer, San Francisco, CA.

Broad, M. L. and Newstrom, J. W. (1992). *Transfer of Training: Action-packed Strategies to Ensure High Payoff from Training Investments.,* Addison-Wesley, Reading, MA.

Cargill, M. (2004). *Teaching in Higher Education,* **9,** 83–98.

Cormier, S. M. and Hagman, J. D. (eds) (1987). *Transfer of Learning: Contemporary Research and Applications.,* Academic Press Inc., San Diego.

Desse, J. (1958). *Transfer of Training: The Psychology of Learning,* McGraw-Hill, New York.

Detterman, D. K. (1993). In *Transfer on Trial: Intelligence, Cognition, and Instruction.* (eds, Detterman, D. K. and Sternberg, R. J.) Ablex Publishing Corporation, Norwood, NJ, pp. 1–24.

Dyson, A. H. (1999). *Review of Research in Education,* **24,** 141–71.

Faerman, S. and Ban, C. (1993). *Public Productivity and Management Review,* **16,** 299–314.

Fogarty, R., Perkins, D. and Barrell, J. (1992). *The Mindful School: How to Teach for Transfer.* Highett, Australia: Hawker Brownlow Education.

Gagne, E. D., Yekovich, C. W. and Yekovich, F. R. (1993). *The Cognitive Psychology of School Learning.* (2nd edn.) New York, HarperCollins College.

Gardner, H. (1991). *The Unschooled Mind: How Children Think and How Schools Should Teach,* Basic Books, New York.

Halpern, D. F. and Hakel, M. D. (2003, July/August). Applying the science of learning to the university and beyond: teaching for long-term retention and transfer. *Change,* pp. 36–41.

Hammer, D., Elby, A., Scherr, R. and Redish, E. (2005). In *Transfer of Learning From a Modern Multidisciplinary Perspective.* (ed., Mestre, J. P.) Information Age, Greenwich, CT, pp. 89–120.

Haskell, R. E. (2001). *Transfer of Learning: Cognition, Instruction and Reasoning,* Academic Press, San Diego, CA.

Hirsch, E. D. (1987). *Cultural Literacy,* Houghton Mifflin, Boston.

Lave, J. and Wenger, E. (1991). *Situated Learning: Legitimate Peripheral Participation.,* Cambridge University Press, Cambridge.

Lister, P. G. (2003). *Social Work Education,* **22,** 125–38.

Marini, A. and Genereux, R. (1995). In *Teaching for Transfer: Fostering Generalization in Learning.* (eds, McKeough, A., Lupart, J. and Marini, A.) Lawrence Erlbaum Associates, Mahwah, NJ, pp. 1–20.

Mestre, J. P. (ed.) (2005). *Transfer of Learning From a Modern Multidisciplinary Perspective,* Information Age, Greenwich, CN.

Misko, J. (1995). *Transfer: Using Learning in New Contexts,* National Council for Vocational Educational Research, Adelaide, Australia.

Noe, R. A. and Colquitt, J. A. (2002). In *Creating, Implementing, and Managing Effective Training and Development: State-of-the-art Lessons for Practice.* (ed., Kraiger, K.) Jossey-Bass, San Francisco, CA, pp. 53–79.

Perkins, D. N. and Salomon, G. (1996a). Learning transfer. In A. C. Tuijnman (ed.), *International Encyclopedia of Adult Education and Training* (2nd edn., pp. 422-27). Tarrytown, NY: Pergamon Press.

Perkins, D. N. and Salomon, G. (1996b). In *International Encyclopedia of Adult Education and Training.* (ed., Tuijnman, A. C.) Pergamon Press, Tarrytown, NY, pp. 422–7.

Phillips, J. (1996). *Accountability in Human Resource Management,* Gulf Publishing Company, Houston, TX.

Ripple, R. E. and Drinkwater, D. J. (1982). In *Encyclopedia of Educational Research* Free Press, New York, pp. 19–48.

Senge, P. M., Kleiner, A., Roberts, C., Ross, R. B. and Smith, B. J. (1994). *The Fifth Discipline Field Book: Strategies and Tools for Building a Learning Organization.* Doubleday, New York.

Thompson, D. E., Brooks, K. and Lizarraga, E. S. (2003). *Assessment & Evaluation in Higher Education,* **28,** 539–47.

Williams, S. D., Graham, T. S. and Baker, B. (2003). *Journal of Management Development,* **22,** 45–59.

2 *Transfer of Learning: Concepts, Theories and Approaches*

This chapter provides an overview of the conceptual background to the transfer of learning. The main approaches are presented in chronological order to give the reader a historical perspective on the development of the concept. Table 2.1 summarises the main approaches to transfer discussed in this chapter. There are three main areas of thinking – the largely discredited formal disciplines approach, the range of theories including the behavioural, cognitive, contextual socio-cultural paradigms and the general theory of transfer, which is informed by all of these. Whilst Table 2.1 is in distinct columns, it must be noted that many approaches are interlinked and will be highlighted in the discussion during this chapter. The chapter concludes with two approaches to transfer, which differ and challenge accepted practice.

Formal disciplines approach

The formal discipline or mental disciplines approach to transfer focused on the transfer of general skills and was based on the training of the mind's faculties (Mayer and Wittrock, 1996). The major purpose of teaching was not the content, but what it trained. This was based on the premise that if the appropriate material was chosen and rote methods of learning employed then the mind would develop a more disciplined intellect – faculties such as memory, attention and judgement were improved and developed. This approach regarded the brain as 'a great muscle' and its strengthening, via mental exercise, was likened to a form of 'mental orthopaedics' (Binet cited in Wolf, 1973, p.207). As the brain gym proponents claim (see for example, Dennison et al., 1995), training in basic mental functions impacts upon new learning.

In classical times the ideal citizen was one who trained via memorisation and imitation in subjects such as astronomy, grammar, logic and mathematics with the intellectual authority of the teacher being paramount. Aristotle's faculty psychology theory was the basis of the mental discipline approach to learning, as it postulated that the mind and spirit were composed of a number of independent faculties of the soul. These functioned to facilitate knowing, reasoning, hungering, feeling and doing. During the Middle Ages the number of faculties grew to include judgement, duty, perception, and conception. The influential philosophers Christian von Wolff and Thomas Reid in the eighteenth century further advanced the notions of faculty psychology. Some 100 years later during the Victorian era, the science of phrenology identified specialised organ areas of the brain associated with specific behaviours and this consolidated the notion that parts of the brain could be exercised and developed by studying. Rippa (1971, p. 208) noted:

> *A mind so sharpened and so stored with knowledge was believed ready for any calling; indeed, it was considered 'trained' and equipped for life. Thus ... transfer of training resulted from*

Table 2.1   Transfer of learning – concepts, theories and approaches

Formal Disciplines Approach	Behavioural Approach	Cognitive and Allied Approaches	Contextual Socio-cultural Approaches
• Training the mind's faculties (e.g. Rippa, 1971)	• **Associationism** Identical elements and similarities approach (e.g. Thorndike, 1901, 1923)	• **Generalisation** Different situations via principles (e.g. Katona, 1940) • **Gestalt** Transfer by insight (e.g. Cox, 1997) • **Information Processing** Processing and accessing of information (e.g. Singley and Anderson, 1989) • **Schema Theory and transfer** Organising information around previously developed ideas (e.g. Cree and Macaulay, 2000) • **Good Shepherd Theory Transfer occurs if shepherded** (Perkins & Salomon, 1990) • **Cognitive Apprenticeships** Modelling, coaching and fading (e.g. Collins, Brown and Newman, 1989) • **Preparation for Future Learning** Transfer as adaptability to new learning situations (e.g. Bransford and Schwartz, 1999)	• **Transfer matrix** Role x Time transfer partnership model (Broad and Newstrom, 1992) • **Socio-technical model** Social and technical factors in work environment (Analoui, 1993) • **Workplace learning** Socio-cultural factors (e.g. Billet, 1992) • **Associated approaches** (e.g. Holton, 1994; Gregoire, Propp and Poertner, 1998) • **Culture and transfer** Impact of culture on transfer (e.g. Lim and Wentling, 1998)
General Theory of Transfer **Using the educational principles we know that work** (Haskell, 2001) **The Transfer Frame** (Vermeulen, 2002)			

sharpening the 'faculties' or powers of the mind, instead of from the specific benefits derived from a particular subject or method of study.

Despite its popularity, research has largely discredited this approach (Perkins and Salomon, 1989). William James, the noted psychologist of the late nineteenth century, demonstrated that memorising poems did not help with the memory learning of poetry and thereby questioned the psychology faculty theories (Kliebard, 1995). His student, Edward Thorndike (cited in Thayer, 1965), developed the connectionism theory and promoted educational methods that were more task-oriented and further discredited the idea that mental discipline had a significant role in transfer of training. However, vestiges of the mental disciplines approach remain. It is believed that certain school subjects can develop common cognitive abilities to be utilised in other subjects and psychological tests are purported to measure mental factors. Rychlak, Nguyen and Schneider (1974) in a series of experiments found that the likeability of a subject could impact upon future learning and postulated that this affective component could be the source of the formal disciplines approach. This is probably analogous to Haskell's (2001) 'spirit of transfer'.

A number of cognitive processing findings have also added to the understanding, but they have emphasised information processing explanations and not student characteristics as a key determining factor. Fong, Kranz and Nisbett (1986) discovered that the learning of probability statistics may generally transfer to everyday reasoning and Lehman, Lempert and Nisbett (1988) indicated that graduate training in one field could impact upon reasoning in another field. In a similar vein Klaczynski (1993) noted that formal reasoning rules can in certain circumstances be acquired in content-specific areas. Therefore, perhaps the formal disciplines approach still has a role to play in explaining the transfer of learning.

Behavioural approach

In response to the formal disciplines approach to transfer, the associationism (or connectionism) explanation was developed, which disputed the notion of general transfer. This was the forerunner to the behavioural explanation, which advocated a technical scientific explanation that emphasised the transfer of specific behaviours. Research undertaken by influential psychologists James (1890), Thorndike and Woodworth (1901) and Thorndike (1923) demonstrated that if subjects were trained on a particular mental or motor task (for example, learning of Latin impacting upon English; hitting a dot with a pencil first with the right hand and then the left) it did not improve performance. Such experiments undermined the formal disciplines explanation. Thorndike and Woodworth (1901, p. 85) stated that the formal disciplines approach erroneously viewed ability as 'something that can be stored in a bank, to be drawn at leisure'.

Associationism was concerned with how learning occurred and defined in terms of stimulus and response through which associations were made; the associations would become weakened or strengthened by the nature and the frequency of the stimulus–response pairings. It was trial and error learning and certain responses dominated due to rewards. Unobservable internal states were not considered to be an important consideration in this learning. This new paradigm considered transfer in terms of identical elements whereby learning of A would facilitate learning of B only if there were common elements between the two. Most of the research was laboratory based, emphasising the role of reinforcement and had only minimal value for the applied classroom setting (Cox, 1997).

The behavioural approach to transfer today is still based upon the issue of similarities and differences in learning and the transfer situation. Ormrod (1998, p. 401) details that transfer is based upon the following four operating principles:

1. 'Maximum positive transfer occurs when stimuli and responses in the two situations are similar.' (For example, learning of two similar languages such as Spanish and Italian.)
2. 'Some positive transfer occurs when stimuli are different but responses are similar.' (For example, when a teacher learns a skill on a course and then uses it in the classroom setting.)
3. 'Negative transfer occurs when stimuli are similar but responses are different.' (For example, a teacher learns the skills associated with student group work but this subsequently interferes with the level of responses needed for individual students.)
4. 'No transfer occurs when stimuli and responses are both different.' (For example, the learning of physical responses will not assist a teacher to develop better instructional techniques for the classroom.)

Cox (1997), however, noted that it is an insufficient explanation for an individual's cognitive developmental level, as reinforcement and transfer history are likely to impact upon responses. Learning was not regarded as a passive process and was more than simply explaining transfer in terms of an input–output model. Indeed, behaviourist explanations promoted considerable debate concerning the role and value of specific transfer. As early as the turn of the twentieth century, Judd (1908) reported that generalisations, and not just specific elements, could transfer from one situation to another whilst Polya (cited in Fogarty and Bellanca, 1995) also noted the importance of a general principles approach (for example, problem solving) to learning transfer. This marked the beginning of the debate between the cognitivists and behaviourists (Cox, 1997).

Generalisation approach and Gestalt theory

The behaviourist position can make contributions to understanding how transfer works, where the specific situations are very similar. If, however, there are only slight similarities, then transfer by generalisation seems a more plausible explanation. The early works of Judd (1908), Katona (1940), Ruger (cited in Mayer and Wittrock, 1996), and Wertheimer (1959) were influential in developing this approach. Katona, for example, demonstrated that if students were taught an understandable principle to solve a problem in a card game, then they would outperform others who had rote learned strategies on one card game only. In situations such as this, if experiences in one situation can be consolidated into generalisations, it holds that transfer may occur. Bower and Hilgard (1981, p.323) summarised the generalisation position in this manner:

A pattern of dynamic relationship discovered or understood in one situation may be applicable to another. There is something in common between the earlier learning and the situation in which transfer is found, but what exists is not identical piecemeal elements, configurations or relationships. One of the advantages of learning by understanding rather than by rote is that understanding is transposable to wider ranges of situations, and less often leads to erroneous applications of old learning.

A key concept is the meaningfulness to the learner, where meaningfulness can bind the situations together (Johnson, 1975). The work of Ebbinghaus (1885) over a century ago clearly demonstrated that material lacking in meaning was rapidly forgotten. The generalisation approach advocates that if learning is meaningful, transfer will occur from one situation to the next if generalisations are mastered and it is acknowledged that they can be applied in different contexts. That is, if situations A and B both require application of the same general strategy (for example problem solving) then transfer can occur. One means of accomplishing this is to encourage students to relate what is new to what is already known.

The Gestalt theory, summarised simply as the 'whole is more than the sum of its parts', is a related, yet more complex explanation of transfer, which built upon the earlier generalisation research findings. It proposed that transfer will occur when an individual recognises similarities or common principles that can be applied in the situations. In essence, the Gestalt position was transfer by insight of specific general skills, if the setting and/or context required similar skills (Cox, 1997). This theory places emphasis upon total patterns of behaviour, however, and rejects the notion that parts can function in isolation. Within the wider context, the emphasis upon principles remains. The significant differing element here to the generalisation approach, is that the response of the individual is also seen as a vital component of the transfer. Hence, the Gestalt approach recognises the importance of a holistic emphasis upon common elements such as intelligence, perception and insight of the individual and the teaching methods as determining factors for transfer. Although acknowledging specific transfer, the Gestalt theory was based upon generalised principles and the importance of the individual's attributes. It has provided a strong foundation for the development of cognitive theory explanations.

Cognitive approaches to transfer

The following sections explore cognitive approaches to the transfer of learning. Beginning with a brief introduction to knowledge, and then moving on to consider information processing approaches to learning and transfer, and in particular the work of John Anderson, followed by a brief overview of schema theory.

In recent times the cognitive approach to transfer has assumed considerable importance and a number of scholarly and multi-disciplinary commentaries have contributed to a deeper understanding of the process (for example, Mestre, 2005). According to the cognitive approach, the transfer of learning is a dynamic and complex phenomenon, driven by cognitive processes. There is a growing convergence among theorists as to how to explain what happens cognitively for a learner facing a new problem or context (Bransford and Schwartz, 1999; Cree and Macaulay, 2000; Haskell, 2001; Smith et al., 1997). These explanations build on understandings of different types of knowledge, and of how these types of knowledge are used and become meaningful to individuals. The term 'knowledge' is used in a broad sense and refers to different types of knowledge, including:

- Conceptual knowledge, also known as: declarative; propositional; replicative and 'knowing that' knowledge – for example, the theory of stress management;

- Procedural knowledge, also known as: applicative; and 'knowing how' knowledge – for example, the steps in managing stress;
- Strategic knowledge, also known as: 'knowing why' knowledge – for example knowing in what circumstances to use stress management techniques; and
- Tacit knowledge, also known as: personal knowledge – own past experiences of stressful situations and how they were dealt with.

When a learner enters a new situation, they bring with them a unique collection of knowledge developed from previous experience and learning. This includes elements of conceptual, procedural, strategic and tacit knowledge. Applying existing knowledge to the new situation is essentially transferring learning (the unique collection of knowledge) to the new situation and this requires new learning. The acquisition of the new learning involves the reconstruction of existing knowledge and of the newly encountered knowledge. This reconstruction occurs through cognitive processing, and involves reflection, generalising and abstraction (Bransford and Schwartz, 1999; Eraut, 1994; Pressley et al., 1987).

Information processing models of learning and transfer

Since the 1950s developments in the information processing capabilities of computers have provided insights and models for human learning. These models of the mind as a computer, provide a way of describing thinking and problem solving. They are known as information processing models of learning. The basic architecture of information-processing models is one of input–process–output. The models include components for encoding, storage and retrieval. In these models the human mind (the computer) takes in information (input), processes it (encoding and storage in the memory) and then the information is later retrieved and applied.

An information-processing model of learning and transfer can be used to explain the theory of identical elements. In this model the training and transfer situations share similar features. Within this explanation, information gained during training is encoded with stimulus cues, which will be recognised and retrieved (the response) in the transfer context. Such explanations are in keeping with the theory of identical elements and account for near, simple, or low road transfer, as described in Chapter 1, but they fail to account for more complex transfer.

Information-processing models have been used extensively by Singley and Anderson (1989) to understand thinking. They have developed an ever-evolving model of how the mind works – that is a model of cognitive architecture, which is called ACT (Adaptive Control of Thought), of which there have been numerous renditions. One ACT* (ACT-STAR) is a general model of skill acquisition. It involves working memory, long-term memory (equivalent to 'declarative knowledge/ knowing that') and production memory (equivalent to 'knowing how/procedural knowledge').

Singley and Anderson (1989) suggested that one of the objections to Thorndike's mechanistic stimulus response conception of the mind was that it was at odds with the traditional notion of transfer, which stressed flexibility and adaptation. In many transfer situations what has been learned is not enough; some adaptation or transformation of existing knowledge is required. Thorndike's conception of transfer did not allow for an intelligent adaptation or reconstruction of what had been learned.

The ACT family of theories were developed in the contexts of learning text processing editors and calculations. Since then, ACT approaches have guided the development of computer-based tutors in mathematics (Ashcraft, 1998). Indications are that these 'tutors' are highly effective. Information processing approaches, such as ACT*, make available to those involved in education and training a theoretical and empirical base for the understanding of cognitive learning, and for understanding how that learning may be adapted or transferred to new situations.

While Anderson's work provides a theoretical base for conceptualising the underlying mechanisms of cognitive skills acquisition and transfer, there are other perspectives from cognitive researchers, which enhance the understanding of transfer.

Schema theory and transfer

This section builds on the information processing approaches to examine schema theory which plays an important role in a number of current approaches to understanding transfer (Cree and Macaulay, 2000; Gagne et al., 1993; Singley and Anderson, 1989).

When a learner faces a problem or new situation they do so with their own existing representations or models of the world. These representations or models were constructed by the learner within earlier experiences or learning situations, and they may be seen as the learner's mental explanations or descriptions of the world. They may be explicit, and the learner is aware of them and can describe them, or they may be tacit and the learner is unaware of their precise form and would have difficulty identifying and describing them. Readers may be familiar with Peter Senge's (1990) work on mental models. Mental models are the assumptions we each carry with us about the world and therefore strongly influence the way we understand the world, and our consequent behaviours.

The learner in a new situation makes sense of it by, what is called 'anticipatory schema', that is, what they already know, their existing models or representations of the world. Transfer of learning occurs when connections are made between existing knowledge, the new situation and the application of the existing knowledge.

Metacognition, which is, being aware of one's own thinking and learning processes, is required to adapt existing schemas to new situations. Positive transfer of learning is dependent on the learner making appropriate connections between existing knowledge and knowledge of the new situation. How the existing knowledge is organised, retrieved and processed has significance for transfer. The transfer problem arises when learners fail to modify schemas, that is, they fail to connect relevant existing learning to new situations. As Cree et al. (1998, p.12) state 'the way in which knowledge is organised through the teaching process is of key importance in terms of developing the learner's own patterns of representing knowledge, and in enabling recall and retrieval strategies'.

The possibility of transfer of learning is enhanced through learners acquiring the habit of thinking about the new situation or problem and identifying in what ways it connects with prior learning or experience. How learners 'think' about the new situation or problem is shaped by the questions they ask themselves.

Cognitive apprenticeships

In the 1990s the concept of cognitive apprenticeships developed by Collins and colleagues became popular in the field of education, particularly within the context of vocational education and training (Brown et al., 1989; Collins et al., 1989). This approach adapts the traditional craft apprenticeship model to one based on the development of cognitive, rather than craft or psychomotor skills. The cognitive apprenticeship approach is a staged approach in which the 'apprentice' develops from being a dependent observer to becoming an independent practitioner (see Figure 2.1).

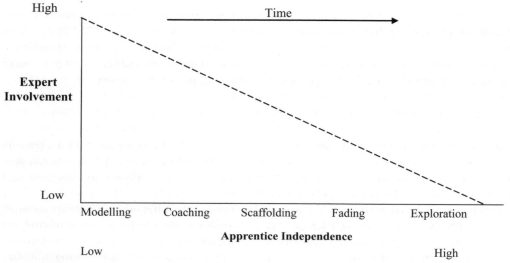

Figure 2.1   Cognitive apprenticeship model

The first stage is one of *modelling* and the expert shares their own internal thought processing with the apprentice, that is, they think aloud. The process is one of progressively moving through the stages of *coaching* in which the expert provides guidance/advice/feedback; *scaffolding*, where the apprentice carries out the task with support from the expert; and *fading*, where the scaffolding or support is removed a stage at a time.

As the learner begins to work independently, they gradually adopt the methods of articulation and reflection. That is, the apprentice is encouraged to make their thinking processes about the task or problem transparent to others. The final stage is the one which has most relevance to more complex transfer and that is the stage of exploration, in which the apprentice is encouraged to learn how to think and/or work in new domains (Beven, 1994; Brown et al., 1989; Collins et al., 1989). The apprentice is being prepared for problem solving and adaptation of their skills and knowledge to new and different situations.

Selected approaches to transfer

WOOLLY APPROACHES OF TRANSFER

Little Bo Peep has lost her sheep
And doesn't know where to find them
Leave them alone and they'll come home
Wagging their tails behind them.

David Perkins and his colleague (Perkins and Salomon, 1990) have used the nursery rhyme 'Little Bo Peep' to create three approaches to transfer: The Bo Peep approach; The Black Sheep approach; and The Good Shepherd approach. Their aim was to help teachers understand when and why transfer of learning occurs, and what can be done to encourage transfer to occur more often. Of particular interest is the Good Shepherd approach to transfer.

The Good Shepherd approach to transfer

The Good Shepherd approach to transfer is that transfer needs to be shepherded for – transfer needs a shepherd or a champion in the learning situation. If 'left alone' it will not happen, if treated as a lost cause, it will not happen. However, if transfer is 'provoked, practised, and reflected on, transfer is easy to achieve' (Fogarty et al., 1992, p.11).

Perkins and colleagues suggest that in teaching for transfer, different strategies are required for low and high road transfer (see Chapter 1). Low road transfer can be achieved by hugging strategies – the learning is close to (hugs) the transfer situation. The teacher keeps the learning task as close to the transfer task as they can. For example, a company is sponsoring a literacy programme in order that employees will be able to read health and safety instructions. The teacher uses the company health and safety instructions in the classroom. High road transfer is more likely to occur where a bridge was created in the learning context to different contexts. Students need to be taught how to build their own bridges as teachers are not always around.

Work-based approaches to transfer

THE TRANSFER MATRIX

Broad and Newstrom (1992) focus on formal training that takes place in order to improve employee performance on the job. They argue for more consultation between trainer, trainee and manager and that the role of transfer manager should be taken on by human resource professionals. They highlighted the importance of both time and participants in the transfer process. Programmes need to be designed to focus on all participants in the training process, as well as what takes place before, during and after the training. Combining these two variables, they developed the Transfer Matrix which provides nine possible role/time combinations (see Figure 2.2).

TIME PERIODS

		Before	During	After
	Manager			
ROLE PLAYERS	Trainer			
	Trainee			

Figure 2.2 The Transfer Matrix; nine possible role/time combinations (Broad and Newstrom, 1992, p.52 – reprinted with permission of the authors)

The transfer matrix enables programme designers to identify who needs to do what, at what stage, to maximise the transfer of training. For each of these combinations they provide a number of useful strategies to enhance transfer, before, during and after training and link these to who is responsible for them – manager, trainer or trainee. Much of their argument is built around Newstrom's (1986) research on the perceptions of trainers regarding barriers to transfer, which identified the key role that managers and trainers play in resolving the barriers to transfer. The three main barriers identified were: lack of reinforcement on the job, interference from the immediate work environment and a non-supportive organisational culture. Reference is also made to the transfer barrier perceptions of executives from Kotter's (1988) study, which echoed the findings of Broad and Newstrom. His findings suggest barriers to transfer often occur in organisations, particularly at the top management level, and that those barriers inhibit change taking place in the workplace after training. Whilst Broad and Newstrom accept that 'trainees must be encouraged to take greater responsibility for their own development of new knowledge, skills and abilities; they are vitally important members of the transfer partnership' (Broad and Newstrom, 1992, p.14), they also identify that the dominant sources of barriers to transfer come from the work organisation and management.

Broad and Newstrom (1992) also draw on the work of Marx (1986) from the drug and alcohol rehabilitation area, to discuss the application of relapse prevention (return to pre-training behaviours) to the transfer area. They suggest that, assuming training has been successful, there are relapse indicators, which appear in the workplace if trainees are not transferring their training. These include:

- A backlog of work or a lack of work resulting in boredom;
- Unsupportive co-workers urging the trainee to revert to old behaviours;
- Other pressures such as restructuring, multi-cultural differences or personal problems, which distract the trainee from focusing on applying their new learning;
- Trainee doubts about using the new skills effectively;
- Little or no management support to use new skills.

THE SOCIO-TECHNICAL MODEL

The 1990s saw a move away from focusing primarily on the psychological influences of transfer, to considering the social-cultural context within which transfer was taking place. The work of Lave and Wenger (1991) and Analoui (1993) is seen as important in this context. Lave and Wenger argue that people learn by entering ongoing 'communities of practice' and gradually work their way into full participation, rather than being trained in isolation of the context in which they are going to be or are working. Analoui focused on the importance of the workplace in terms of facilitating transfer of learning. He suggested that traditionally little attention had been paid to the social-cultural context of the work environment and how this could either facilitate or inhibit transfer of learning. Transfer of learning is regarded as a process which is dependent on learning not just the tasks or skills, but also on learning about and understanding the social-cultural context within which these tasks and skills are to be applied. To meet both these needs, Analoui advocated a model which highlights the relationship between the complexity of the task to be learned and the location of training.

Analoui (1993) argues for a socio-technical model of transfer where there is a move away from a focus on tasks, to an emphasis on the role of socialisation in the workplace. He regards training as including three aspects.

1. 'Systematic processes which are concerned with some form of planned and controlled, rather than random learning experience;
2. Changing the behaviour, skills and attitudes of people as individuals and as members of social work groups;
3. Improvement of both the present and the following job performance (effective transfer) and enhancement of the effectiveness of the organisation in which the individual or group works' (Analoui, 1993, p.5).

Analoui (1993, p.5) also suggests that 'the overall effectiveness of the trainees may not necessarily be related solely to the improved task performance but could also be due to their social competence skills'.

He discusses the location of training and the importance of social processes in the learning process, in particular 'the socialisation processes which occur both during and after the training programme' (Analoui, 1993, p. 10). Analoui sees transfer as a complex process including the individual's experiences, expectations and ability, as well as the learning experience per se and the work environment provided by the organisation.

Analoui (1993) indicates that as the process of transfer extends into the workplace it is difficult to 'completely harness and bring under control' (p.20) other factors which may contribute to effective or ineffective transfer. To minimise the impact of these factors, he advocates an experiential learning approach as it focuses on the learner, giving them a certain amount of autonomy. He also supports the use of learning contracts as it improves the transfer back to the workplace.

One of Analoui's main assertions is that the low amount of transference experienced may be due to the traditional focus on task learning, which has ignored the social learning processes that take place on training programmes. He suggests that 'some of these social learning processes may have an undoing effect on the task-related learning and the process of transfer as a whole' (Analoui, 1993, p.52–53). These social learning processes are not only related to the training environment, but also include social and cultural expectations of the workplace and the interpersonal skills needed to remain effective as a member of the organisation after training.

The question of training location is, according to Analoui, dependent on the nature and complexity of the job. In essence, this means that the more complex the job the further away from the workplace the training should be. However, he argues that a combination of on-the-job and off-the-job training may be best in terms of transferring learning to the workplace. Therefore, off-the-job training is for more complex jobs, such as managerial positions, and for those people who are to be 'change agents' on return to the workplace. In addition, he advocates that in any off-the-job training there needs to be time set aside to prepare people for their return to work.

These arguments culminate in a taxonomy of the socio-technical model of transfer and types of training situations (see Figure 2.3). Figure 2.3 suggests that there is usually a combination of task and social learning processes present in training programmes. Analoui (1993) maintains that the closer the training programme is to the actual workplace, the stronger the influence of social learning becomes and with that the potential for effective transfer is increased.

The taxonomy shown in Figure 2.3 is divided further by considering where the trainee is going after the programme. This is seen as important in terms of the training methods adopted. For example, a trainee going to a new job in a new workplace, would, according to this taxonomy benefit from an off-the-job training situation which focuses on task-related learning.

More recent research by Bresnen et al. (2003) and Boreham and Morgan (2004) has added credence to the notion of both communities of practice and the role of social practices within organisations in terms of facilitating transfer. Bresnen et al.'s research within the construction industry highlighted that the social patterns and practices of the organisation are key determinants in not only capturing knowledge, but also effect transfer and learning in project environments. Similar conclusions were reached by Boreham and Morgan in a three-year longitudinal study within an oil refinery and petrochemical manufacturing complex.

WORKPLACE LEARNING

The main workplace factors identified in the literature as facilitating transfer include direct supervisor support (Brinkerhoff and Montesino, 1995; Broad and Newstrom, 1992; Garavaglia, 1993; Gregoire et al., 1998; McSherry and Taylor, 1994; Mmobuos, 1987; Noel and Dennehy, 1991; Xiao, 1996), socio-cultural factors (Analoui, 1993; Billet, 1992, 1994; Bresnen et al., 2003; Boreham and Morgan, 2004; Buckley and Caple, 1996; Lave and Wenger, 1991), social support

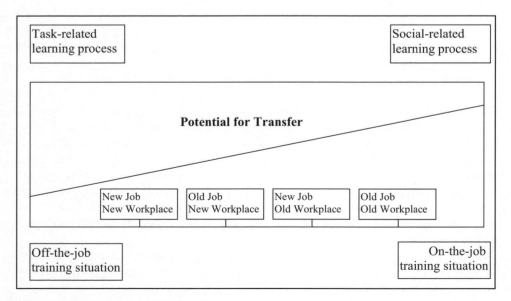

Figure 2.3   A taxonomy of the socio-technical model of transfer and types of training situations (Analoui, 1993, p.123 – reprinted with permission of the author)

(McGraw, 1993; Tracey et al., 1995), continuous learning culture (Boreham and Morgan, 2004; Tracey et al., 1995) and transfer of training climate (Boreham and Morgan, 2004; Bresnen et al., 2003; McGraw, 1993; Tracey et al., 1995).

Noel and Dennehy (1991) argue for a partnership to be formed with the learner's supervisor. This includes gaining the supervisor's input into the course, meeting with them and the learner prior to and after the course. Brinkerhoff and Montesino (1995), Garavaglia (1993) and McGraw (1993) support this, but argue for wider management support, not just from the immediate supervisor. Their main reason for this is that the wider work environment may impact on the learner's opportunity to transfer their knowledge and skills. McSherry and Taylor (1994) suggested that running supervisor workshops, facilitated by the course deliverers, should be held to facilitate the transfer process. The work environment may also be quite unpredictable, particularly when dealing with a government agency such as the Accident Compensation Corporation (ACC) or the Ministry of Education. Xiao (1996), in her study of the transfer of training in the electronics industry in Shenzhen, China, argues along similar lines, suggesting that supervision is the most crucial factor in the work environment for transfer to take place. She states (p.59) that 'when training programmes improve the workers' potential, they also bring about changes in workers' expectations of themselves and of the organisation'. In order to then realise this potential the organisation needs to be ready for these changes in expectations.

The issue of training location is considered by a number of authors (Analoui, 1993; Billet, 1992, 1994; Buckley and Caple, 1996; Lave and Wenger, 1991). Billet (1992) argues that it is important to have training based in the workplace, so as not to neglect the socio-cultural factors of the workplace. The basis for this argument is that new attitudes learned at off-site training, for example, may not be compatible with the actual workplace – so a degree of workplace reality needs to be introduced at some stage during the training course.

Stuart (1992) suggests that it is of benefit to only train some of a work group at one time, as it enables a constant refresher to take place for those who have already completed the course. This overlap of students also enables informal mentoring to occur, with past students assisting those on the course. Stuart (1992) also indicated that peer support groups facilitate the transfer of learning, in the sense that they may provide some continuity to relationships established during training programmes.

This notion ties in with the concepts of organisational culture and climate, which Tracey et al. (1995) considered as important for transfer of learning to take place. In their study of supermarket managers, they were considering why training works. In particular, they considered the work environment, which they divided into transfer of training climate and continuous-learning culture. The 'transfer of training climate refers to the perceptions about characteristics of the work environment that facilitate or inhibit the use of trained skills and behaviours' (p.242). This is seen to include, for example, managerial and peer support for training and development, and performance appraisal systems that account for behaviour and skills acquired in formal training programmes. 'A continuous-learning environment is one in which organisational members share perceptions and expectations that learning is an important part of everyday life' (p.241).

McGraw (1993) also emphasised the importance of organisational culture in terms of trying to redress some of the re-entry problems encountered by training participants when returning to the workplace. His research findings whilst focusing on outdoor management development programmes also have wider applicability. He identified three particular problems often associated with returning to work – the 'return from space effect', the 'hangover effect' and the 'widows and orphans effect' (McGraw, 1993, pp.58–9). The 'return from space effect' takes place when the trainee has developed and changed but the workplace has not. This often means that it is difficult for trainees to re-integrate back into the work environment and there may be resistance from colleagues to suggested changes made by the trainee. Similarly, some training participants may be bored and under-stimulated on their return to the workplace, or they may have realised that they have the potential to achieve more than they had previously thought possible. These feelings are associated with the 'hangover effect'. Feeling on one's own after training, is like being widowed or orphaned, as the support of the training group and trainer is not necessarily available once back at work.

The need for a supportive internal climate and strong champions for change within organisations were also found in the research by Bresnen et al. (2003) and Boreham and Morgan (2004). Boreham and Morgan, in particular, advocate a socio-cultural approach to organisational learning where 'individual and social learning are mutually constitutive' (2004, p.321). This moves away from the more individualistic approach to learning, and their research demonstrated that there needs to be a common object for employees to be working towards for there to be learning as an organisation and for transfer ultimately to take place.

However, contrary to the prevailing research on the importance of the transfer climate in facilitating the transfer of learning, some research is showing that transfer is taking place in spite of a supportive transfer climate (Leberman, 1999; Pate et al., 2000).

ASSOCIATED RESEARCH

Mosel (cited in Broad and Newstrom, 1992) argued that three conditions must be present for effective transfer to take place. The training content must be applicable to the job, the trainee must learn the content and the trainee must then be motivated to change their job behaviour to apply that new learning. The emphasis was on the trainee, who was responsible for ensuring that transfer took place, assuming that the training was relevant and successful.

The role of support systems within the workplace was discussed by Nadler (cited in Broad and Newstrom, 1992), who suggested that the trainee needed to be supported in order for transfer to take place. He argued that the level of management support was crucial and that the timing of training also played a part in ensuring successful transfer. Byham, Adams and Kiggins (cited in Broad and Newstrom, 1992) in their study on supervisory skills, suggested that three factors support the transfer of training involving all the participants in the transfer process. Firstly, that trainees have acquired new skills – the trainer's responsibility. Secondly, that they have the confidence to try their new-found skills on the job – the trainee's responsibility. And thirdly, that the new skills are positively reinforced on the job – the manager's responsibility.

A review of some of the management, education and psychology literature since 1986, shows that the key factors discussed with respect to transfer of training are timing – (before, during and after) and the people involved – (the trainer/training deliverer, the trainee and the work organisation).

Baldwin and Ford's (1988) consideration of the transfer of training literature and Ford and Weissbein's (1997) follow-up review provide a useful overview of the research in the area to that date, as well as suggesting future directions for research. Baldwin and Ford provided a model of the transfer process, which considers three aspects of the transfer process – training inputs, training outputs and conditions of transfer. The training inputs are classified into trainee characteristics (ability, personality and motivation), training design (principles of learning, sequencing and training content) and work environment (support and opportunity to use). Training outputs are associated with learning and retention, whilst the conditions of transfer focus on the generalisation and maintenance of what was learned. The Ford and Weissbein review updated findings in the areas of the definition and operationalisation of transfer, task characteristics, training design, trainee characteristics and work environment factors.

More specific studies have covered some of the following areas:

- General ability of the learner (Bereiter, 1995; Rouiller and Goldstein, 1993), including student background (Castaldi, 1989);
- Motivation to learn (Holton, 1996; Mbawo, 1995; Noe and Colquitt, 2002; Wlodkowski, 2003);
- Self-efficacy (Ford et al., 1998; Mbawo, 1995) and self-esteem (Mink et al., 1993);
- The ability to take risks (Friedman, 1990; Robinson, 1992);
- Internal locus of control and relapse prevention (Haccoun, 1997; Haccoun and Saks, 1998; Tziner et al., 1991).

A more recent review of the transfer of training research between 1989 and 1999 by Cheng and Ho (2001) has added new dimensions to the three areas identified by Baldwin and Ford (1988) and the Ford and Weissbein (1997) reviews. Under trainee characteristics they identified, for example, achievement striving and trainee-control-over-training, and under work environment the concept of transfer climate.

Whilst not a review of the literature per se, the research by Barnett and Ceci (2002) provides a detailed review of the history of the transfer of learning and highlights some of the key issues associated with transfer from an education and psychology perspective. Barnett and Ceci (2002) argue that achieving far transfer is very difficult to assess, because it takes place after people have left the formal education system. They suggest that because the success of transfer depends on the similarity between the context of training and testing (application), it is important for educators to know what knowledge needs to be learned at school so it is useful later in life. To address this situation Barnett and Ceci developed 'a taxonomy of transfer content and context containing nine dimensions, three of content and six of context' (2005, p. 298).

Other general overviews of the subject are provided in research by Mbawo (1995), Holton (1996), Gregoire et al. (1998), Machin (2002) and Noe and Colquitt (2002). Mbawo identified five factors affecting the transfer of learning drawing on previous literature. These factors were individual/trainee characteristics, organisational climate, training design, learning styles and trainer strategies/facilitation style. She also interviewed six trainers from private, public and academic institutions to identify the methods used by them to enhance the transfer of learning. Her findings were grouped into the three time phases of the transfer process. The preparations before training involved manager/trainee interviews, trainee expectation assessments and thorough training needs assessments. During training, the use of experiential learning methods was prevalent, with case studies and story-telling being provided as examples. Voluntary participation was seen as important and learning contracts were also used. After training, feedback, both individual and collective is valued, and should be coupled with short-term and long-term action planning. Some trainers included on-the-job observation post-training and questionnaires to industry were also used. In spite of being able to provide a number of strategies to enhance the transfer of learning, there was still concern expressed by the trainers about the level of transfer actually taking place.

Holton (1996) approaches the transfer question from an evaluative perspective and argued for a new human resources development evaluation research and measurement model. He suggested that the Four-Level Evaluation Model (Kirkpatrick, 1994), together with its modifications by various other authors, had 'received incomplete implementation and little empirical testing' (Holton, 1996, p.6). Furthermore, he stated (p.8) that 'there is a complex system of influences on training outcomes that must be measured if training is to be accurately evaluated'. Following on from this statement, his model, therefore, considers the influences on learning, performance outcomes and organisational results, based on the individual, the environmental (contextual) elements, as well as individual and organisational facilitative factors.

Gregoire et al. (1998) approached the subject from a social work perspective and reviewed the literature associated with the transfer of training in the social work, educational and organisational psychology, management and organisational behaviour areas. They concluded that there was little empirical literature available on the transfer of training back to the workplace. However, the literature reviewed indicated that individual attributes, the training curriculum and the work environment influenced the transfer process.

The focus of Gregoire et al.'s (1998) research was on the role of the supervisor in facilitating transfer back to the workplace. The findings suggested that course participants received little support from their supervisors once back at work. This lack of support is attributed to the low level of impact the training subsequently had on the workplace. These findings are not new, with Baldwin and Ford (1988), Garavaglia (1993) and McSherry and Taylor (1994) for example, coming to similar conclusions. One of the implications of these findings is aptly summerised by Gregoire et al. (1998, p.15).

In order to reap the benefits of training, organizations must be committed to, and take responsibility, for training. It is probably not sufficient to have a motivated supervisor. Ultimately, the agency's commitment to training emanates from upper management. The importance that upper administration places on training most certainly influences the supervisor's willingness and ability to enhance the benefit of training.

The long-term study (1989–1993) of Feldstein and Boothman (1997) exemplifies the interdependence between learner, programme design and workplace, and as such makes an important contribution to understanding the key determinants of transfer success. Although their study was concerned with training computer application personnel, their eight key facilitative factors related to attitudes and behaviour are important factors to consider in all training settings. They are as follows:

1. Learners reported exploration or use of software prior to training;
2. Before the training they had a clear idea of how to apply the skills used in class;
3. After training, they had three or more practice sessions per week;
4. After training they had many ways to apply the skills on the job;
5. The learners perceived that the supervisors had reasonable expectations for performance change after training;
6. The learners perceived that the supervisor had adequate knowledge and understanding of how the learner would use the software;
7. Learners felt supported by management in their learning and growth using the software; and
8. Learners observed that management had noticed and communicated about productivity and process changes since the training.

Two recent books provide very helpful overviews of the transfer of learning and training. The chapters by Noe and Colquitt (2002) and Machin (2002) in Kraiger's (2002) book *Creating, Implementing, and Managing Effective Training and Development,* are particularly useful in terms of maximising the transfer of training. Noe and Colquitt focus on the importance of motivation for training by both the individual and the organisation, arguing that training motivation is the key to learning transfer. They conclude by stating that 'the research findings are unequivocal: individual and work environment characteristics influence learning and transfer' (Noe and Colquitt, 2002, p.75).

Machin's chapter considers how to optimise the transfer of training by providing a model of the transfer of training based on the work of a number of authors. In essence, it is an extension of the transfer matrix suggested by Broad and Newstrom (1992), and integrates other research culminating in an integrated transfer of training model based on training inputs and outcomes, as well as transfer outcomes. He acknowledges that despite being aware of the factors that maximise transfer, 'training will sometimes be delivered in an organizational context that is not supportive, with trainees who have little motivation or interest, and with a focus on short-term outcomes that do not contribute to desirable team or organizational outcomes' (Machin, 2002, p.296).

Mestre's (2005) book *Transfer of Learning From a Modern Multidisciplinary Perspective* approaches the topic of transfer of learning from a range of psychological and physics education perspectives. He argues that the most useful way of looking at transfer is from what he calls an 'expanded view', where researchers have considered factors such as the socio-cultural environment (Lave and Wenger, 1991). Most of the chapters focus on the formal education setting and are concerned with assessment and transfer. However, the chapters by Schwartz et al. (2005) and Rebello et al. (2005) highlight the importance of the people who 'do the transferring' – the training participants or students.

CULTURE AND TRANSFER

There has been a growing literature about the relationship of culture and learning (for example, Ogbu and Simons, 1998; Rosinski, 2003), however, little has been documented about the relationship of culture to transfer. As discussed above, there is a significant literature base explaining how the psychological, cognitive and social factors relate to transfer, but minimal research and theory development has occurred to explain the significance of culture (Sarkar-Barney, 2001). It is acknowledged, however, that culture does have a significant part to play in understanding transfer. Haskell (2001, p. 143) states that 'cultures transmit norms that influence student learning is not new to anthropologists who study education, understanding how cultures specifically influence and shape transfer is new. The anthropological research that does exist needs to be gleaned for its specific relevance to transfer'. Some studies are beginning to explore the issue, but more is needed (for example, Hannon and D'Netto, 2005; Horwath and Shardlow, 2001; Sarkar-Barney, 2001; Teaching PJB Associates, 2004; Yamnill, 2001).

As societies become increasingly multi-cultural and education and training delivers to increasingly diverse groups, it is apparent that there is an urgent need to research the relationship between culture and transfer, as well as develop a more adequate understanding of this relationship. Lim (1999) for example noted that with globalisation, there is an increasing need to consider transfer of training from a cross-cultural perspective. That is, there is a need to define a model of transfer that reflects the generally established principles of transfer, but also incorporates all key dimensions (such as cultural factors) that are specific to that context. Western models of learning and transfer will not always be sufficient.

There are a number of issues related to culture that can provide an indication about this relationship. Hofstede (1984; 1991) provides some information about the importance of cultural values and how these can impact upon learning settings. He identified four important factors that conceptualise trainer–trainee (or teacher–learner; boss–worker) relationships. If there is a value or norm match between the key players on these criteria, then there is potential for sustained, valued relationships. For example, if the dimensions of power–distance (that is either perceived high or low distance), capacity to deal with uncertainty (for example being innovative rather than rule-bound), individualism/collectivism, and masculinity (for example assertiveness)/femininity (for example, concern for others) are concordant for trainers and trainees from diverse cultures, then it is likely that effective learning relationships could develop. Sarkar-Barney (2001) noted the importance of Baldwin and Ford's (1988) model for other cultural contexts, but emphasised the significance of cultural values impacting upon transfer. The implications of these findings for research and practice are significant.

Another focus which provides an insight into the nature of transfer and culture, relates to the growing awareness of the importance of culture and ethnicity in adult education theory (Brookfield, 1995). It has also highlighted the importance of understanding intra-group differences. According to Brookfield this has two implications: to incorporate diverse views about learning and teaching, the Western adult learning tradition will need to be revised *and* practices will need to be developed that encourage the teaching of the group by someone from within that group.

Cross-cultural contacts and how such relationships evolve to a satisfactory level also need to be considered. Once again little is known about how individuals function in a new culture, although it has significant implications when teachers/instructors and learners are involved. Inter-cultural competency can readily be obtained by many individuals, but it remains unclear how this is operationalised in settings (Ptak et al., 1995). A number of studies, Benson (1978) for example, have identified specific behaviours and predictors of inter-cultural competency such as language skills, attitude, socially appropriate behaviours, friendliness and mobility. Both Taylor (1994) and Jacobson (1996) hypothesised about a theoretical framework to explain these phenomena, but agreed there was a need for more understanding and the explicit specification of strategies. Hammer, Gudykundst and Wiseman (1978) postulated that there were three important factor constellations: the ability to deal with psychological stress, the establishment of interpersonal relationships and the ability to effectively communicate. In conclusion, it was suggested that the development of what was termed a 'third cultural perspective' enabled an individual to interpret host culture experiences.

Undoubtedly, however, as one moves towards an inter-cultural identity there is an adaptive process (Kim and Ruben, 1988; Oberg, 1960). Jacobson (1996) noted that many earlier attempts to explain the process of inter-cultural competence were flawed, as internal phenomena were the primary focus, with the specific situational and social domains being overlooked. His approach identified situated cognition as the crucial determinant for learning culture '. . . ways of knowing of how to make sense of a situation, and how to interact in ways that will make sense in that situation, are inextricably linked to that situation' (p.16).

A number of experts have recognised the specific difficulties of cross-cultural barriers in learning. For example, language barriers (Dillon, 1993), societal value differences (Adler, 1986), learning style differences (Hofstede, 1991) and technical differences (Lim and Wentling, 1998) have all been identified as training problems. Haskell (2001) recommended the incorporation of culture as an important variable into a comprehensive model of the learning and transfer process. Similarly, Xiao's (1996) study in China emphasised that transfer is indeed an international concern.

Some attention has also been directed at the role of local and immediate socio-cultural factors in transfer of training. Analoui (1993), Billet (1992, 1994), Boreham and Morgan (2004), Bresnen et al. (2003) as well as Lave and Wenger (1991), have, for example, emphasised not only the technical aspects of training, but also the role of social processes in transfer. On-site training maximised opportunities for this to occur as it was more likely to match the task and social requirements of the setting and make re-entry less problematic (Analoui, 1993; McGraw, 1993). Congruence of training intentions and the work site was embodied within the research of Tracey at al. (1995) who identified the importance of a facilitative transfer climate and a continuous learning culture on site. Managerial and peer support as well as work appraisal opportunities within an ongoing learning environment, provided the context for inter-related social and task learning opportunities. Rouillier and Goldstein (1993) and Noe (1986) identified behavioural cues from supervisors and peers as important post-training transfer environment issues, whilst Tannenbaum and Yukl (1992) added that transfer can be actively discouraged if there is ridicule from peers in the workplace. These developments were insightful, but did not go far enough in explaining the pervasive nature of national culture upon transfer.

The relatively recent growth of cultural psychology also highlights the significance of culture in the daily lives of individuals. In many respects this explanation is an extension of the situated learning approach but, as Ratner (1997) has suggested, there is a need to broaden this explanation. What he believes is required is an emphasis upon the impact of concrete social structures on psychological phenomena such as learning (and transfer), rather than the narrow, symbolic and mentalistic interpretation of a 'situation'. Culture is more than shared meanings – it *exists* in our daily activities (for example, child rearing, education), influences power/authority/status relationships (for example, group authority), and allocates division of labour that categorises behaviour (for example, teacher learns from the teacher trainer). The thesis is, that as we engage in these practical and social activities, psychological functions are formed; that is, culture significantly determines, for example, perception, self concept, gender behaviour, thinking, emotions, personality, and these in turn interact with the culture and modify it. Thus cultural activity and psychological phenomena depend upon and sustain one another. What can be implied from Ratner's approach is that learning and transfer will be mediated by the cultural activities, which in turn will impact upon the activities. The implication of his work is that the identification of the cultural imperatives is a priority, if we are to facilitate learning for impact.

Lim and Wentling's (1998) work in the area of culture and transfer is one of the very few explanations explicitly considering the importance of cultural factors in transfer of training, basing their international model of transfer of training on the earlier works of Baldwin and Ford (1988) and Brinkerhoff and Gill (1994). Their approach identified the learning environment (training and trainee characteristics), cultural differences (language, social, technical and learning) and work environment (encompassing work and people factors) as the features most affecting the transfer of training. Their research noted that cultural differences were found to significantly affect transfer of training. Overall, it was a dynamic explanation with the three major domains interacting with each other, although there was a general directional flow starting with the learning environment, through to cultural differences and then work environment. Lim (1999) argues that individual, organisational and cultural needs assessment procedures will facilitate effective training by being mirrored in training design with diverse teaching strategies.

Two small-scale studies (Hynds, 1997; Tufue, 1998), very similar in design, related the issue of culture to the nature and value of in-service support for transfer of training. The Hynds's study surveyed Pakeha (New Zealand European) participants, whilst the Tufue investigation surveyed Polynesians resident in New Zealand. Hynds noted that support was very often related to an individual's professional goals. The Tufue study had similar results, but more attention was directed to the value of support as a collaborative goal. Additional research needs to be undertaken to extend the findings of these studies and to consider the wider implications of how transfer and culture are linked.

Preparation for future learning

Brandsford and Schwartz (1999) have reconceptualised transfer of learning as 'Preparation for Future Learning' (PFL). They are more optimistic than others of the potential for learning to transfer. In looking at the research evidence, which is damning of transfer, Bransford and Schwartz identified problems with how transfer is tested for, and difficulties with the original learning.

Typically tests for transfer are conducted in an artificial setting such as a psychology laboratory or in a controlled workplace environment. The test of transfer takes place immediately following the 'training' or 'learning' situation. The learner is presented with the transfer task or problem and expected to directly apply what they have just learned. Bransford and Schwartz (1999) refer to this as direct application (DA). They use the analogy of a jury; in order that the jury is not contaminated by outside influences the jury is shut away or sequestered to reach its decision. The learner is sequestered when testing for transfer. In order to test the learning and transfer the learner is isolated, and is not provided with the options of utilising other resources such as:

- Asking colleagues;
- Consulting their notes or texts from the course;
- Trial and error;
- Feedback from others; and
- Opportunities to revise.

The situation is described as sequestered problem solving (SPS). Bransford and Schwartz suggest that the combination of DA and SPS testing of transfer is responsible for the pessimism about transfer. The SPS approach does not reveal the hidden potential for transfer. They quote a study from Singley and Anderson (1989) to illustrate this. The study examined the influence learning one text editor had on learning a second text editor. The initial test for transfer showed that learning one text editor had not resulted in an enhanced ability to learn the second text editor. However, subsequent testing on day two revealed evidence that learning one text editor had enhanced the learning of the second text editor. This example demonstrates that one-off SPS tests may be too weak to measure the effects of original learning and practice. This also highlights the importance of time and place when considering transfer.

Bransford and Schwartz's alternative approach to transfer is PFL. Their PFL theory is highly relevant for knowledge-rich settings such as workplaces, educational institutions and community organisations. Bransford and Schwartz regard PFL as another theory of transfer, which complements rather than displaces other theories, which they see as being useful in some contexts and for some reasons. They wanted a shift in perception so that the measure of transfer of learning is about assessing the ability of a learner to learn in new and real situations, such as workplaces. They point out that when a person starts a new job they are not expected to know everything required for adaptation to the new setting. An employer will want employees who know how to learn and make use of available resources (colleagues, workplace manuals, books, CD-ROMs, the Internet, and so on), to pose questions and to adapt to the workplace. 'The better prepared they are for future learning, the greater the transfer (in terms of speed and or quality of new learning)' (Bransford and Schwartz, 1999, p.68).

They provide an example of novice teachers. Using the SPS and DA approach, the novice teachers would be assessed on their application of what they had learned on their course. The assessment would be a one-off assessment at the end of the course. In contrast, if a PFL approach was used, the assessment would focus on how the novice teacher shaped the new environment for their own future learning by, for instance, setting in place arrangements for peer feedback, organising resources and drawing up questions. The PFL perspective is that an appropriate measure of transfer focuses on the learner's abilities to learn new information and to make connections with prior experience. 'One determinant of the course of future learning is the questions people ask about the topic, because these questions shape their learning goals' (Bransford and Schwarz, 1999, p.69).

Bransford and his colleagues see understanding transfer as important to understanding learning and by implication to developing effective teaching practices. The ability of students to transfer learning, can provide teachers with valuable information for the evaluation and improvement of teaching and learning. Earlier we discussed the theory of identical elements and theories emphasising generalisation. Bransford in the book *'How People Learn'* (2000) emphasises that the most effective transfer of learning comes from providing learners with a balance of specific examples (identical elements) and general principles. The time spent on gaining understanding has consequences for transfer, which is different from time spent on rote learning or memorisation.

A general theory of transfer

Haskell (1998) focused on transfer in instructional settings and regards learning and transfer as being inextricably linked; transfer is the very essence of learning. He argues that we have not related what we know about learning to transfer and unless we do this we will continue to have an incomplete understanding of the concept. Contrary to many others (see for example, De Corte, 1996) Haskell viewed learning as a special case of transfer since it consisted of all the understanding processes essential for changes in thinking and behaviour. He defined transfer of learning as 'our use of past learning when learning something new and the application of that learning to both similar and new situations' (Haskell, 2001, p. xiii). However, he elaborated that the literature is replete with such definitions and these do not acknowledge transfer as a most pervasive issue that appears deceptively simple.

Numerous theories, as discussed in this chapter, have attempted to explain transfer and although these expanded understanding somewhat, ironically they have developed it as one of the most complicated and pervasive issues in psychology and education. He believes this complexity and theoretical confusion has resulted in a collapse of the concept and engendered considerable debate and confusion in the literature. There remain immense difficulties in answering the questions 'what do we mean by transfer?' and 'how do we transfer?' He states: 'research findings over the past nine decades clearly show that as individuals, and as educational institutions, we have failed to achieve transfer of learning on any significant level' (Haskell, 2001, p. xiii). It is a paradox that, although transfer is acknowledged as fundamental to learning, it is rarely achieved when we want it and yet achieved without our efforts at other times.

The issue of transfer of training has been of considerable interest to many practitioners and theory builders involved in education, psychology and training (Haskell, 2001), but it has been enmeshed in this uncertainty and a preoccupation with specific transfer strategies. He believes it is remarkable that fundamental theoretical and research issues remain unanswered and when they are answered, they are only limited attempts to address these in a systematic manner. Haskell (2001) argues that an integration of transfer research, theory and practice is necessary and noted that the resurgence of interest in the applied contexts in the industry, training and education arenas has made this even more imperative. What is required is a coherent and united research framework that permits the development of a general, systematic and over-arching instructional model of transfer incorporating all the competing approaches, but based upon effective learning principles.

Haskell's approach has drawn upon research findings and effective practices in education, psychology, training and neurology to develop what he terms an encompassing and integrated theory of transfer. He has outlined 11 widely accepted educational principles and related them to a general theory of teaching for transfer. These principles are as follows:

- Acquiring a large knowledge base and expertise in the areas that transfer is required;
- Acquiring knowledge from other areas outside the primary area, which at first may seem irrelevant and useless (for the time being), but could be useful at a later date in developing analogies for the new domain;
- Understanding the history and theoretical bases of transfer;
- Acquiring a 'spirit of transfer' or a motivation to transfer;
- Learners need to understand what transfer is and how it works;
- Developing an orientation to think in transfer terms because significant transfer does not occur automatically. Learners need to develop thinking and encoding skills to facilitate transfer (for example, 'What does this mean for me? What are my experiences in relation to it?');
- Developing transfer support systems and creating cultures of transfer;
- Developing theoretical knowledge about the area of transfer which must take into account existing personal theories about the area and be corrected if necessary;
- Utilising practice and drill opportunities;
- Allowing time for the learning to 'incubate'; for it does not occur instantaneously, and
- Using the experiences of people (system thinkers, discoverers, inventors, literary experts) who are exemplars of transfer of training.

Haskell believes that there is neither a short cut approach to transfer, nor a step-by-step formula and that the adoption of these principles is important if we want to move beyond the metacognitive level of simple transfer. To understand the concept and facilitate instructional transfer it is important to identify different levels and move beyond the simplistic 'near–far' dichotomy, leading him to develop a broad and varied description of the different levels of transfer, shown in Table 2.2. This typology is a relativistic approach based upon the similarity judgements of the individual. That is, what is near transfer to one person may be far for another and hence the importance of what is in the mind of the perceiver.

Table 2.2   Typology of transfer levels (adapted from Haskell, 2001)

LEVEL	NAME	TRANSFER DESCRIPTION
1	Non-specific transfer	This refers to all learning – all learning has been connected to past learning.
2	Application transfer	Applying what one has learned to a specific situation.
3	Context transfer	Applying what one has learned to a slightly different situation (e.g., recognising something in one context and then in another).
4	Near transfer	Transferring to new situations that are closely similar (e.g., learning a skill and then using part of that learning to develop another skill).
5	Far transfer	Applying learning to situations that are quite dissimilar.
6	Creative transfer	In the interaction between the new and old situation something new is created.

In addition to this, Haskell indicated that these levels need to be considered in relation to the varieties of transfer of learning – the knowledge categories (content, procedural, declarative and strategic) and the specific transfer process types (conditional, theoretical, general, literal, vertical, lateral, reverse, proportional and relational). This provides a somewhat complex typology that enables an evaluation of 'level X knowledge type X transfer type' with person X.

Empirical research needs to be undertaken to validate Haskell's ideas, but it is important to recognise his contribution to our understanding. Firstly, he has provided a principle-based and integrative framework for understanding a complex issue that recognises the very important dynamic between learning and transfer. It moves beyond the traditional 'teach-for-transfer' appeal and is based upon what we already know about classroom and everyday learning. His approach is derived from a combination of applied educational and cognitive research, as well as Haskell's own experiences. Furthermore, it provides ample information about how to develop learning environments to ensure transfer becomes a way of thinking and knowing. He does not claim to have developed a 'new' theory or set of practices, but promotes the idea that what we know about theory, research and practice in instruction needs to be integrated if we are serious about instructional transfer. His plea is for a more principled and coherent strategic application of the knowledge base.

Other ways of looking at transfer

Transfer is generally considered as the link between learning and performance and when this does not take place there is a transfer gap. This chapter has considered different ways of facilitating transfer so that this gap does not eventuate.

Research by Vermeulen (2002, p. 369) suggests that rather than transfer being seen as a 'from ... to model', it needs to be seen as a two–way process where 'transfer is a recurrent process of learning and performance, that takes place both in the training context and the work context'. She argues that by reframing transfer in this way there is no transfer gap, but rather a transfer membrane which separates and connects the training and work contexts that continuously interchange. If this is the case there are implications for both training design and the workplace, as both learning and performance will take place in both contexts.

Brinkerhoff and Apking (2001) argue that transfer as presented in this chapter is not enough and for high impact learning to take place, what they term leveraged transfer needs to occur. Leveraged transfer is where 'learners focus on the strategic few performance improvements that are most likely to lead to achievement of key business goals' (p.17). Their approach is based on the premise that learning drives performance, as it is performance rather than just ability, which leads to most impact from training.

Summary

The various approaches, theories and concepts discussed in this chapter provide an overview of the myriad of research in the area of transfer of learning. What is clear from the discussion is that there still remains much debate surrounding the transfer of learning, often couched in the particular philosophical approach adopted. What cannot be disputed is that in all cases we are dealing with people and how they transfer their learning from one context to another. To this end a certain amount of cognitive processing takes place and is important. This links with the Boud and Walker model introduced in Chapter 1. In essence the approaches presented emphasise particular aspects of the model, in terms of focusing on, for example, the learner, or the actual learning experience or the work environment. Key to all of these in the final analysis is the ability of the learner to learn from their experience and transfer it to the context which is appropriate for them. The case studies which are presented in Chapters 4, 5 and 6 draw on different approaches, focusing on those that are most relevant to the particular research. In all of the case studies, however, the experience of the learner and their opinions on the transfer of learning, is at the forefront.

References

Adler, N. J. (1986). *International Dimensions of Organisational Behaviour*, Kent, Boston, MA.
Analoui, F. (1993). *Training and Transfer of Learning*, Avebury, Aldershot.
Ashcraft, M. (1998). *Fundamentals of Cognition*, Addison-Wesley Educational, New York.
Baldwin, T. T. and Ford, J. K. (1988). *Personnel Psychology*, **41**, 63–105.
Barnett, S. M. and Ceci, S. J. (2002). *Psychological Bulletin*, **128**, 612–37.
Barnett, S. M. and Ceci, S. J. (2005). In *Transfer of Learning From a Modern Multidisciplinary Perspective*. (ed., Mestre, J. P.) Information Age, Greenwich, CN, pp. 295–312.
Benson, P. G. (1978). *International Journal of Intercultural Relations*, **2**, 21–37.
Bereiter, C. (1995). In *Teaching for Transfer: Fostering Generalization in Learning*. (eds, McKeough, A., Lupart, J. and Marini, A.) Lawrence Erlbaum Associates, Mahwah, NJ, pp. 21–34.
Beven, F. (1994). In *Cognition at Work* (ed., Stevenson, J.) National Centre for Vocational Education Research, Adelaide, pp. 217–43.
Billet, S. (1992). *Studies in Continuing Education*, **14**, 143–55.
Billet, S. (1994). *Vocational Aspects of Education*, **46**, 3–16.
Boreham, N. and Morgan, C. (2004). *Oxford Review of Education*, **30**, 307–25.
Bower, G. H. and Hilgard, E. R. (1981). *Theories of Learning*, Prentice Hall, Englewood Cliffs, NJ.
Bransford, J. D., Brown, A. L. and Cocking, R. R. (eds) (2000). *How People Learn: Brain, Mind, Experience and School*, National Academy Press, Washington DC.
Bransford, J. D. and Schwartz, D. L. (1999). *Review of Research in Education*, **24**, 61–100.
Bresnen, M., Edelman, L., Newell, S., Scarborough, H. and Swan, J. (2003). *International Journal of Project Management*, **21**, 157–66.
Brinkerhoff, R. O. and Apking, A. M. (2001). *High Impact Learning: Strategies for Leveraging Business Results*

From Training, Perseus Publishing, Cambridge, MA.

Brinkerhoff, R. O. and Gill, S. J. (1994). *The Learning Alliance: Systems Thinking in Human Resource Development*, Jossey-Bass, San Francisco.

Brinkerhoff, R. O. and Montesino, M. U. (1995). *Human Resource Development Quarterly*, **6**, 263–74.

Broad, M. L. and Newstrom, J. W. (1992). *Transfer of Training: Action-packed Strategies to Ensure High Payoff From Training Investments.*, Addison-Wesley, Reading, MA.

Brookfield, S. D. (1995). *Becoming a Critically Reflective Teacher*, Jossey-Bass, San Francisco.

Brown, J. S., Collins, A. and Duguid, P. (1989). *Educational Researcher*, **18**, 32–42.

Buckley, R. and Caple, J. (1996) *One-to-one Training and Coaching Skills*, Kogan Page, London.

Castaldi, T. M. (1989). *Lifelong Learning*, **12**, 17–19.

Cheng, E. W. L. and Ho, D. C. K. (2001). *Personnel Review*, **30**, 102–18.

Collins, A., Brown, J. S. and Newman, S. (1989). In *Knowing, Learning, and Instruction: Essays in Honour of Robert Glaser*. (ed., Resnick, L. B.) Lawrence Erlbaum, Hillsdale, NJ, pp. 453–94.

Cox, B. (1997). *Educational Psychologist*, **32**, 41–55.

Cree, V. E. and Macaulay, C. (eds) (2000). *Transfer of Learning in Professional and Vocational Education*, Routledge, London.

Cree, V. E., Macaulay, C. and Loney, H. (1998). The Scottish Central Research Unit, Edinburgh.

De Corte, E. (1996). In *International Encyclopedia of Developmental and Instructional Psychology*. (eds, De Corte, E. and Weinert, F. E.) Pergamon, Oxford, pp. 33–43.

Dennison, G., Dennison, P. and Teplitz, J. (1995). *Brain Gym for Business: Instant Brain Boosters for On-the-job Success*, Edu-Kinesthetics, Inc., Venture, CA.

Dillon, L. S. (1993). *Training and Development*, **47**, 39–43.

Ebbinghaus, H. (1885). *Memory: A Contribution to Experimental Psychology*, Teachers College, Columbia University, New York.

Eraut, M. (1994). *Developing Professional Knowledge and Competence*, Falmer Press, London.

Feldstein, H. D. and Boothman, T. (1997). In *Transferring Learning to the Workplace*. (ed., Broad, M. L.) ASTD, Alexandria, VA, pp. 19–33.

Fogarty, R. and Bellanca, J. (1995). In *Best Practices for the Learner-centred Classroom: A Collection of Articles*. (ed., Fogarty, R.) IRI/Skylight Pub, Palatine, IL, pp. 73–100.

Fogarty, R., Perkins, D. and Barell, J. (1992). *The Mindful School: How to Teach for Transfer*, Hawker Brownlow Education, Highett, Australia.

Fong, G. T., Krantz, D. H. and Nisbett, R. E. (1986). *Cognitive Psychology*, **18**, 253–92.

Ford, J. K. and Weissbein, D. A. (1997). *Performance Improvement Quarterly*, **10**, 22-41.

Ford, K., Smith, E. M., Weissbein, D. A., Gully, S. M. and Salas, E. (1998) *Journal of Applied Psychology*, **83**, 218–33.

Friedman, B. A. (1990). *Training & Development Journal*, **December,** 17–19.

Gagne, E. D., Yekovich, C. W. and Yekovich, F. R. (1993). *The Cognitive Psychology of School Learning*, Harper Collins College, New York.

Garavaglia, P. L. (1993).*Training & Development Journal*, **October**, 63-8.

Gregoire, T. K., Propp, J. and Poertner, J. (1998). *Administration in Social Work*, **22**, 1–18.

Haccoun, R. R. (1997). *Applied Psychology: An International Review*, **46**, 340–4.

Haccoun, R. R. and Saks, A. M. (1998). *Canadian Psychology*, **39**, 33–51.

Hammer, M. R., Gudykundst, W. B. and Wiseman, R. L. (1978). *International Journal of Intercultural Relations*, **11**, 65–88.

Hannon, J. and D'Netto, B. (2005). In *17th Biennial Conference of the Open and Distance Learning Association of Australia*, Adelaide.

Haskell, R. E. (1998). *Reengineering Corporate Training: Intellectual Capital and the Transfer of Learning*, Quorum Books, Westport, CO.

Haskell, R. E. (2001). *Transfer of Learning: Cognition, Instruction and Reasoning*, Academic Press, San Diego, CA.

Hofstede, G. (1984). *Cultures' Consequences: International Differences in Work-related Values*, Sage Publications, Beverly Hills, CA.

Hofstede, G. (1991). *Cultures and Organizations: Software of the Mind*, McGraw-Hill, New York.

Holton, E. F. I. (1996). *Human Resource Development Quarterly*, **7**, 5–21.

Horwath, J. and Shardlow, S. (2001). *European Journal of Social Work*, **4**, 29–38.

Hynds, A. (1997). In *Wellington College of Education*, Wellington College of Education, Wellington, NZ.

Jacobson, W. (1996). *Adult Education Quarterly*, **47**, 15–28.

James, W. (1890). *Principles of Psychology*, Holt, New York.

Johnson, N. F. (1975). *Journal of Verbal Learning and Verbal Behavior*, **14**, 17–29.

Judd, C. H. (1908). *Educational Review,* **36,** 42–8.

Katona, G. (1940). *Organizing and memorizing: Studies in the psychology of learning and teaching.* Columbia University Press, New York.

Kim, Y. and Ruben, D. (1988). In *Theories of Intercultural Communication.* (eds, Kim, Y. and Gudykundst, W. B.) Sage, Newbury Park, CA, pp. 299–321.

Kirkpatrick, D. (1994). *Evaluating Training Programmes: the Four Levels,* Berrett Koehler, San Francisco, CA.

Klaczynski, P. A. (1993). *Journal of Educational Psychology,* **85,** 679–92.

Kliebard, H. M. (1995). *The Struggle for the American Curriculum,* Routledge, New York.

Kotter, J. P. (1988). *The Leadership Factor,* Free Press, New York.

Kraiger, K. (ed.) (2002). *Creating, Implementing, and Managing Effective Training and Development. State-of-the-art Lessons for Practice,* Jossey-Bass, San Francisco, CA.

Lave, J. and Wenger, E. (1991). *Situated Learning: Legitimate Peripheral Participation,* Cambridge University Press, Cambridge.

Leberman, S. I. (1999). The Transfer of Learning from the Classroom to the Workplace: A New Zealand Case Study. Unpublished PhD, Victoria University of Wellington, Wellington, p. 304.

Lehman, D., Lempert, R. and Nisbett, R. E. (1988). *American Psychologist,* **43,** 431–42.

Lim, D. (1999). *Performance Improvement,* **38,** 30–6.

Lim, D. and Wentling, R. M. (1998). *International Journal of Training and Development,* **2,** 17–28.

Machin, M. A. (2002). In *Creating, Implementing, and Managing Effective Training and Development: State-of-the-art Lessons for Practice.* (ed., Kraiger, K.) Jossey-Bass, San Francisco, CA, pp. 302–30.

Marx, R. D. (1986). *Training and Development Journal,* **January,** 54–7.

Mayer, R. and Wittrock, M. (1996). In *Handbook of Educational Psychology.* (eds, Berliner, D. and Calfee, R.) Prentice Hall, London, pp. 47–62.

Mbawo, E. (1995). *Training and Management Development Methods,* **9,** 729–44.

McGraw, P. (1993). *Asia Pacific Journal of Human Resources,* **3,** 52–61.

McSherry, M. and Taylor, P. (1994). *The International Journal of Human Resource Management,* **5,** 107–19.

Mestre, J. P. (ed.) (2005). *Transfer of Learning From a Modern Multidisciplinary Perspective,* Information Age, Greenwich, CN.

Mink, O. G., Owen, K. Q. and Mink, B. P. (1993). *Developing High Performance People – the Art of Coaching,* Addison-Wesley Publishing Company, Reading, MA.

Mmobuos, I. A. (1987). *Journal of European Industrial Training,* **1,** 13–16.

Newstrom, J. W. (1986). *Journal of Management Development,* **5,** 33–45.

Noe, R. A. (1986). *Academy of Management Review,* **11,** 736–49.

Noe, R. A. and Colquitt, J. A. (2002). In *Creating, Implementing, and Managing Effective Training and Development: State-of-the-art Lessons for Practice* (ed., Kraiger, K.) Jossey-Bass, San Francisco, CA, pp. 53–79.

Noel, J. L. and Dennehy, R. F. (1991). *Journal of European Industrial Training,* **15,** 17–18.

Oberg, K. (1960). *Practical Anthropology,* **7,** 179–82.

Ogbu, J. and Simons, H. (1998) *Anthropology and Education Quarterly,* **29,** 155–88.

Ormrod, J. E. (1998). *Educational Psychology: Developing Learners,* Prentice Hall, Upper Saddle River, NJ.

Pate, J., Martin, G., Beaumont, P. and McGoldrick, J. (2000). *Journal of European Industrial Training,* **24,** 149–57.

Perkins, D. N. and Salomon, G. (1989). *Educational Researcher,* **18,** 16–25.

Perkins, D. N. and Salomon, G. (1990). The Science and Art of Transfer. Retrieved 15 June 2001 from www.learnweb.harvard.edu/alps/thinking/docs/trancost.htm.

Pressley, M., Snyder, B. L. and Carglia-Bull (1987). In *Transfer of Learning: Contemporary Research and Applications* (eds, Hagman, J. D. and Cormier, S. M.) Academic Press, Toronto, Ontario, pp. 81–119.

Ptak, C., Cooper, J. and Brislin, R. (1995). *International Journal of Intercultural Relations,* **19,** 425–53.

Ratner, C. (1997). *Cultural Psychology and Qualitative Methodology: Theoretical and Empirical Considerations,* Plenum Press, New York.

Rebello, N. S., Zollman, D. A., Allbaugh, A. R., Engelhardt, P. V., Gray, K. E., Hrepic, Z. and Itza-Ortiz, S. F. (2005). In *Transfer of Learning From a Modern Multidisciplinary Perspective.* (ed., Mestre, J. P.) Information Age, Greenwich, CN, pp. 217–50.

Rippa, S. A. (1971). *Education in a Free Society,* David McKay Company, New York.

Robinson, D. W. (1992). *Journal of Applied Recreation Research,* **1,** 12–36.

Rosinski, P. (2003). *Coaching Across Cultures,* Nicholas Brealey, London.

Rouiller, J. Z. and Goldstein, I. L. (1993). *Human Resource Quarterly,* **4,** 377–90.

Rychlak, J., Nguyen, D. and Schneider, W. (1974). *Educational Psychology,* **66,** 139–51.

Sarkar-Barney, S. (2001). Extending a Transfer of Training Framework to Include the Role of National

Culture. Unpublished Doctoral, Bowling Green State University, Bowling Green, OH.

Schwartz, D. L., Bransford, J. D. and Sears, D. (2005). In *Transfer of Learning From a Modern Multidisciplinary Perspective*. (ed., Mestre, J. P.) Information Age, Greenwich, CN, pp. 1–52.

Senge, P. M. (1990). *The Fifth Discipline: The Art and Practice of the Learning Organisation,* Double Day, New York.

Singley, M. K. and Anderson, J. R. (1989). *The Transfer of Cognitive Skill,* Harvard University Press, Cambridge, MA.

Smith, E., Ford, J. K. and Kozlowski, S. W. J. (1997). In *Training For a Rapidly Changing Workplace: Applications of Psychological Research*. (eds, Quinones, M. A. and Ehrenstein, A.) American Psychological Association, Washington DC, pp. 89–118.

Stuart, P. (1992). New directions in training individuals. *Personnel Journal*, September, 86-101.

Tannenbaum, S. I. and Yukl, G. (1992). *Annual Review of Psychology, 43,* 399–441.

Taylor, E. W. (1994). *Adult Education Quarterly, 44,* 154–74.

Teaching PJB Associates (2004). *Immigation and Cross-cultural Teacher Training. New Perspectives for Learning – Briefing Paper*. Retrieved 10 January 2006, from www.pjb.co.uk/npl/bp1.htm

Thayer, V. T. (1965). *Formative Ideas in American Education,* Dodd, Mead and Company, New York.

Thorndike, E. L. (1923). *School Sociology, 17,* 165–68.

Thorndike, E. L. and Woodworth, R. S. (1901). *Psychological Review, 8,* 247–61.

Tracey, J. B., Tannenbaum, S. I. and Kavanagh, M. J. (1995). *Journal of Applied Psychology, 80,* 239–52.

Tufue, R. (1998). Wellington College of Education, Wellington, New Zealand.

Tziner, A., Haccoun, R. R. and Kadish, A. (1991) *Journal of Occupational Psychology, 64,* 167–77.

Vermeulen, R. C. M. (2002). *Journal of European Industrial Training, 26,* 366–74.

Wertheimer, M. (1959). *Productive Thinking,* Harper and Row, New York.

Wlodkowski, R. J. (2003). *New Directions for Adult and Continuing Education, 98,* 39–47.

Wolf, T. H. (1973). *Alfred Binet,* University of Chicago Press, Chicago, IL.

Xiao, J. (1996). *Human Resource Development Quarterly, 7,* 55–73.

Yamnill, S. (2001). *Factors Affecting Transfer of Training in Thailand*. Unpublished Doctoral, University of Minnesota, Minneapolis, MN.

3 *The Role of Learning in Transfer*

This chapter discusses key ideas, principles and strategies of learning as they relate to transfer and sets the scene for the case studies which follow in Chapters 4–6. What we argue is that for the adult learner to maximise the transfer of learning, develop personally and professionally, and be able to deal with change, we need to have an understanding of the factors that influence development and theories of change. By having an understanding of these we can then incorporate a range of learning approaches appropriate to the specific context, which will enhance the developmental process over time. This chapter discusses the characteristics of adult learners, professional development and relevant theories of change with respect to transfer. A number of key learning approaches important for transfer are reviewed and linked to the role they play in facilitating this process. These approaches include experiential learning, action learning, situated learning, collaborative learning and transformative learning (see Figure 3.1 for a summary of this).

The three case studies all involve adult learners and draw on concepts and theories of adult learning discussed within this chapter. Sarah's case study involved a group of adult learners enrolled in a diploma designed to meet the needs of their organisation; Lex's case study involved teachers whose learning was in the context of a professional development programme; the participants in Stephanie's study were enrolled in a distance-learning business degree.

Adult learners

Earlier chapters have shown how transfer and learning are inextricably linked. New learning comes from the transfer of previous learning to a new situation. Transfer is the use of learning in new and different situations. The authors all work with adult learners, and have written this book for those engaged in teaching and learning with adult learners. While there is not universal agreement as to definitions or theories of learning, adult learners and adult learning, there are some approaches which have wide acceptance in the field of adult education and training. In an attempt to develop a distinct theory of adult learning Knowles (1975, 1984a, 1984b) advocated the use of the term andragogy. Initially, he sought to identify the differences between adult and children's learning. A summary of how Knowles contrasted the pedagogy and andragogy is shown in Table 3.1.

While many adult educators welcomed a term that was specific to adult teaching and learning and the term still enjoys some popularity today, it never gained universal acceptance and the differences claimed between how adults and children learned have been contested (Imel, 1995). Later, Knowles reconceptualised pedagogy and andragrogy as a continuum of learning on which both children and adults could be placed on any point and which was changeable according to context. For instance, a young child may be a self-directed learner as they construct a fort, but may revert to being other-directed for classroom maths. An adult

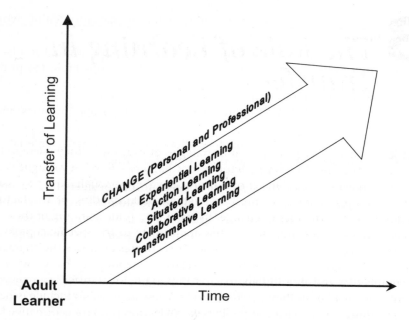

Figure 3.1 Adult learning, change, approaches and transfer of learning

Table 3.1 Knowles's view on the differences between the learning of children and adults (adapted from Knowles, 1975)

	Children's learning/Pedagogy	Adult learning/Andragogy
Concept of learner	• Other-directed. • The teacher is responsible for deciding what, when, how learning will occur and how it will be assessed.	• Self-directed. • The learner is responsible for deciding what, when, how learning will occur and how it will be assessed.
Role of learner's experience	Little attention or value is placed on the learner's experience. The emphasis is on the expertise of the teacher, to be derived from the text, and of other acknowledged experts.	The learner's prior learning and experience is seen as a rich resource for learning. The learner is encouraged to make connections between prior experiences and the learning task.
Readiness to learn	Instruction is designed to provide a standardised, step-by-step programme of learning. Learners progress systematically through the steps.	Learning is determined by the need to know or learn for real life problems or tasks.
Orientation to learning	Subject or discipline focused. Learning for the future.	Performance centred. Want to be able to apply what they have learned within their current roles.

may be self-directed in relation to a personal project such as digital story telling, while they may need to be other-directed in terms of learning to swim.

Andragogy was defined as a technology that should drive the education of adults, 'the art and science of helping adults learn' (Knowles, 1980, p. 43). He identified four key principles:

1. Adult learners need to be involved in the planning and evaluation;
2. Learning activities should be based upon experiential learning opportunities (including mistakes);
3. Adults are most keen when there is immediate relevance of the content material;
4. Adult learning is problem-centred rather than content-oriented.

In other words the process of the instruction needs to be considered as an important component of the programme. Case-studies, role plays and simulations, for example, were important approaches and the instructor was regarded as a facilitator, rather than lecturer. Knowles (1985) recommended that the following strategies would best meet the needs of adults:

- Setting a co-operative learning climate;
- Creating mechanisms for mutual planning;
- Undertaking a diagnosis of learner needs and interests;
- Planning learning objectives on the basis of the identified needs;
- Designing sequential activities to meet the objectives;
- Selecting appropriate methods, materials and resources; and,
- Evaluating the learning and re-diagnosing learning needs.

Similar points were raised by Castaldi (1989), who, in her work with adult learners attending university, draws on the work of Freiere (1970) who suggested that it is important to learn about the backgrounds of the students prior to commencing teaching. She states that 'students who are involved in academic pursuits for the first time or after a long hiatus will actively draw upon relevant experiences in order to construct a viable model which can be used to achieve immediate goals' (p.18).

CHARACTERISTICS OF ADULT LEARNERS

Numerous appraisals of Knowles's work have been undertaken and a number of theorists have built on his ideas about adult learning and adult learners (Boud and Griffin, 1987; Brookfield, 1986; Brandes and Ginnes, 1986; Brundage and MacKeracher, 1980; Cross, 1981; Knowles et al., 2005; Knox, 1986; Merriam and Caffarella, 1998; Mezirow, 1981; St Clair, 2002). Most would now agree that effective learning and teaching practices apply to all learning and are not specific to adult learning, but that the degree and the frequency of these may be more marked in adult learning. Commonly identified characteristics of adult learners include:

- The tendency with maturation to move from being other-directed to being *self-directed*;
- That with ageing can come a wealth of *prior experiences* and learning which may be a rich resource for learning;
- An individual's experiences become crucial to their *sense of self* as they age;
- An individual's *readiness to learn is linked* closely to their social roles;
- As an individual ages their perspective on time shifts from one with a future orientation to one which emphasises *immediate application*;

- As individuals mature they tend to prefer learning, which is *problem-centred,* rather than theoretical or content-centred.

These characteristics are not universal to all adult learners, but commonly found in adult learners. An appreciation of the characteristics of adult learners and of approaches based on andragogy, provide adult educators and trainers with a basis for designing programmes for adult learners. The design needs to recognise that the learners will be self-directed, bringing with them a wealth of prior experiences and learning, that their experiences have shaped their sense of self, that their time is valuable and they will be wanting to apply their learning to real life problems. This is similar to what Boud and Walker advocate in the preparation and experience stages of their model (see Figure 1.1), where the personal foundation of experience the learner brings is of prime importance.

Professional development

The terms professional development, continuing education and in-service training have been used extensively and often inter-changeably. In general, these terms refer to a broad range of activities that contribute to knowledge, skills and behaviours of an individual once the initial training has been completed. For this book, the definitions adopted by the OECD (1998) in discussing teacher professional development will be adopted. Professional development will refer to *any activity* that develops an individual's skills, knowledge, expertise or other characteristics and includes personal study, reflection and formal course participation. In-service education and training are part of professional development, but are *specific* terms indicating that the professional participates in identifiable learning activities, often within the context of a course or workshop.

WHAT IS PROFESSIONAL DEVELOPMENT?

Although one of the hallmarks of a profession has been the acquisition of specialised knowledge and competencies, Eraut (1994) describes professionalism in terms of an ideological foundation – there is an emphasis upon the values of service, trustworthiness, integrity, autonomy and reliable standards. He notes it is not easy to define the nature of a professional in precise terms because specific ideal occupational types are exclusionary. The literature on professional development and learning, although extensive, is somewhat limited in scope with regards to how professionals best learn and apply such learning. There is a growing literature (for example, Cheetham and Chivers, 1996; Eraut, 1994) on descriptions of competencies, expected outcomes of professional learning and strategies for achieving these requirements, but little written about how training is specifically linked to impact on-the-job.

Indeed the Dreyfus and Dreyfus (1986) model of skill acquisition suggests that training, although initially important for deliberative action, is of secondary importance to learning by experience. They believe that the process of moving from a novice to expert is determined by the level of intuition and deep tacit understanding gained on the job, rather than the rigid deliberate application of taught rules. This does imply, however, that the initial training together with experience permit the professional to proceed from guidelines and conscious deliberative approaches to a more holistic understanding of the situation, which becomes the precursor to the intuitive non-analytical expert performance. So it is experience that is the catalyst for expert functioning, but questions remain about the model. What transfer techniques are initially important for the professional to gain the rules and plans and what experiences are best for moving the professional from novice to expert performance (Eraut, 1994)?

Schön (1983) critiqued the rational-technicist point of view as being too simple and not relating to practice and he developed his widely known alternative approach, the reflective practitioner. His thesis is that a professional's work is creative and when problems arise experience and reflection are used to help solve the issues arising. He termed this 'reflection-in-action'. Schön noted that the life of a professional depends upon knowing-in-action (that is having skilled behaviour), but reflection-in-action occurs when the situation is not normal. When this occurs the professional asks 'what is this?', 'what got me into this fix?' and then 'what can I do about it?' One of the key dimensions here is the role of time (Eraut, 1994). Some situations can be reflected upon whilst others require a very speedy response. Another problem relates to the nature of reflection – Schön never really articulated what this was. Reflection-on-action (also considered by Kolb, 1984 and Dewey, 1938) was the process of making sense of the experience after it had occurred and possibly learning something from it to add to the repertoire of experience. Once again time is an important issue to consider here and questions remain about the differences between reflection-in-action (which usually requires speedy response) and reflection-on-action (which is more deliberative). Recent research by Leberman and Martin (2004) would suggest that the depth of reflection may increase with distance from the training course.

Cheetham and Chivers (2000) have acknowledged that the different models for professional learning and development – apprenticeship, technical-rationalist, reflective practice, functional competence and personal competence – each have strengths and limitations and that a more holistic approach is required. Their model consists of four key competency components each having various constituent parts: functional (for example, performance of tasks), personal or behavioural (for example, ability to work with others), knowledge/cognitive (for example work-related knowledge and using it) and values/ethics (for example, professional codes of conduct). Over-arching meta-components (for example, communication, self-development, creativity) are also a part of this model. The meta-competencies along with the four competencies and their constituents interact to produce the outcomes.

The work on the professional development models and learning has provided considerable information on the phases, processes and products of professional learning and practice. What is missing, however, is a detailed understanding of how the training (whether this be academic or work-based) can best be used to ensure that experience, reflection and deliberative action, becomes part of the professional practice and therefore facilitates transfer of learning. McDonald (2005), in discussing teacher education, indicates that there should be a close relationship between education, training and experience with a central importance given to transfer of training technology. The literature on transfer of learning can approach many of these issues and provide clarification for improved professional development. It can, for example, provide insight into a number of the issues detailed above. Such as:

- Establishing the means of teaching reflection so that it is used on the job;
- Identifying the types of 'experiences' that would ensure expert intuitive action occurs; and
- Locating strategies to teach deliberative decision-making so that it impacts upon specific client needs.

One of the key issues for in-service training relates to the transfer of learning (OECD, 1998). Ford (1994) noted that transfer of training is very much related to change and in specific terms requires an orientation towards:

- A clear identification of what is to be changed;
- The nature of the changed behaviour and settings;
- What could prevent the change; and
- The degree of maintenance of change.

It is important then, and indeed relevant to the above discussion about professional development, to identify how in-service or any professional education programme and transfer of learning are related. That is, if in-service training is deemed effective, does it not obviously imply improved performance on-the-job? Although one should imply the other (and indeed Haskell (2001) subsumes learning under transfer of learning), they have often been considered complementary procedures with a somewhat different focus (McDonald, 2002). Learning and understanding of ideas has been more readily related to immediate in-service outcomes, whilst transfer of learning has been associated with sustained quality implementation of the in-service ideas on-the-job. McDonald urges a synthesis of the two notions – effective in-service and transfer of learning – as this would enhance teacher development considerably. With this in mind, it is important then to locate the in-service approaches and strategies that can achieve this objective.

With the increasingly multi-cultural workforce it is also important to ensure that professional development is culturally responsive. Wlodkowski (2003) argues that participants in professional development courses need to be motivated to learn for transfer to have a chance to take place. If participants are uncomfortable with the process of delivery then they may disengage from the learning process at an early stage. He argues that deliverers of professional development need to be culturally responsive by using a framework for instruction consisting of four key aspects:

1. 'Establishing inclusion;
2. Developing attitude;
3. Enhancing meaning;
4. Engendering competence' (2003, p.40).

Wlodkowski concludes that by adopting this framework, using peer coaching, action research and providing organisational support, the potential for transfer for all participants, irrespective of their cultural background, is maximised.

Change theories

Transfer of learning needs to be understood in terms of an understanding of the change process, particularly with regard to motivation as mentioned above, the adoption of ideas, attitudes and behaviours and the context of the change. Behavioural change refers to developmental growth in knowledge/feelings/skills and is a personal experiential process, not merely an event occurring before institutional change, as shown in Boud and Walker's model (see Figure 1.1). There are numerous explanations about individual change and how this occurs in settings (see for example, Bandura, 1977; Fullan, 1991; Hall and Hord, 1987; Havelock and Zlotolow, 1995;

Lewin, 1951; Reigeluth and Garfinkle, 1994; Rogers, 1995), but much of the important and often cited literature arises from the field of education. Linking knowledge of change theories, models and concepts with how transfer of learning occurs can assist in understanding how best to transfer (Bellanca, 1996).

Ferguson (1980) identified four different types of change and undoubtedly these intersect with the types of transfer previously discussed. *Change by exception* refers to an individual making one change to an existing belief structure (for example, a racist accepts another person of different race as a friend). *Incremental change* is when change occurs so slowly that it is unnoticed. An example of this is when a teacher initially uses computers very reluctantly, but then subsequently values the use in the classroom. Changes that result in an opposite point of view are known as *pendulum changes*; a lecturer who previously utilised a lecture format presentation moves to a problem-based learning approach is evidence of this type of change. *Paradigm change*, the type of change most frequently associated with a mind set change of beliefs and behaviours, is more likely to be transformational and impact upon organisational approaches. Explaining training in terms of a social constructivist perspective instead of a knowledge deposit (*tabula rasa*) orientation is a paradigm change required to facilitate the transfer of learning.

There are two basic approaches to understanding change: the Newtonian framework and the dynamic paradigm. The former approach implies designed, planned change, which is organised, rational, efficient and clear. Dynamic change, however, defines the process as more than intended and tends to be non-linear, less predictable, and manageable. The implication being, that the system needs to be read well and be prepared for designed and emergent change. Arising from these two paradigms, a number of theories and explanations explaining how individuals and organisational change occurs have been developed (see for example, Bandura, 1977; Ellsworth, 2000; Fullan, 1991; Havelock and Zlotolow, 1995; Imel, 2000; Lippit et al., 1958; Rogers, 1995). In surveying these approaches, a range of themes can be identified: there is an emphasis upon forces and resistances to change (for example, motivation, knowledge, resources), roles and relationships (for example, role of managers) and the actual processes of change (for example, diagnosis and identification of issues, persuasion techniques, decision-making, implementation, evaluation). By assuming an eclectic perspective seven distinct phases of change can be identified from these approaches – awareness that there is a problem, identification of the problem or opportunity, collection of data, analysis of data, planning the change, implementation and evaluation.

One particular theoretical approach that has often attracted interest in explaining transfer in terms of facilitation and barriers to change is Lewin's (1951) force-field model. He viewed change as a process of unfreezing thoughts and behaviours that mitigate the need for change, moving ideas and behaviours into new channels and then refreezing them when functional and productive again. These new patterns remained in this state of equilibrium until there was a need to change again. Lewin believed it was easier to bring about change by reducing the forces against change, than by increasing the forces for the change. To accomplish this it was necessary to determine the needs in the context that were threatened by the proposed change and then find ways to meet these concerns. A force-field analysis could assist this process by identifying the driving and restraining forces for change.

A number of other commentators have emphasised the importance of the links between individual and context of change. Imel (2000), in discussing the role of the change agent noted the importance of being pro-active and providing a strategy for change, teaching the individual the necessary skills for change *and* working within the context to achieve the change. In a similar vein, Bellanca (1996) argued that the organisation and the individual need to develop an ethos that learning is a preparation for life, with an expectation that the professional development programmes imply on-the-job application of ideas. As a means of facilitating this, learning tasks (for example, authentic activities) and processes need to be implementation focused. He further noted that individual change and organisational change were woven like a fine rug – pull one thread and damage to the whole carpet occurs.

In a more specific analysis of the process, Ellsworth (2000) surveyed the literature and formulated a synthesis framework model that accounted for individual change in context. Overall his framework can best be understood in the following terms. The change agent communicates the innovation to 'another' and this is accomplished via a change process within a particular context, which may contain resistances that disrupt or modify the innovation. He has outlined this as a number of recursive steps and draws upon the existing approaches in the literature to explain the process, namely:

- Initiating the change and understanding the overall process (for example, Fullan, 1991);
- Understanding the operation of the systemic components inside and outside the organisation to appreciate its needs (for example, Reigeluth and Garfinkle, 1994);
- Planning and guiding future efforts related to the change process (for example, Havelock and Zlotolow, 1995);
- Committing to a plan and acting (for example, Hall and Hord, 1987);
- Identifying the resistances (for example, Zaltman and Duncan, 1977) and dealing with them (for example, Rogers, 1995) and/or rectifying deficiencies in the change environment to more readily accept the change (for example, Ely, 1990).

A number of commentators (for example, Surry et al., 2004) have identified the range of conditions that underlie this process of change, but as Surry et al. note, the relative significance of such variables is likely to vary. The following conditions are a summary of what many of these commentators have defined as the critical variables to innovate successfully.

1. Dissatisfaction with the current status;
2. Change needs to be perceived as a human activity and not a technological activity;
3. There should be a fostering of continued improvement in knowledge and skills to ensure innovation occurs;
4. There needs to be an understanding that change is a process not an event;
5. Acceptance, valuing and learning from failure is sanctioned;
6. Resources are made available;
7. All stakeholders participate meaningfully;
8. Leadership and commitment is visible and change encouraged by such people;
9. Rewards and incentives are available for the innovators; and
10. Time is made available for changes to happen.

Individuals and organisations often find change difficult and yet what we know is that innovation is one of the cornerstones of a modern society. As indicated by the above discussion, transfer of learning and change are two sides of the same coin; they are both intimately related to learning, involve innovation and a human condition that is continually unfolding.

Approaches to adult learning

EXPERIENTIAL LEARNING AND ACTION LEARNING

The literature concerning experiential and action learning together with the concept of 'the reflective practitioner' (Schön, 1983) are important issues to consider with regard to transfer. Experiential learning is introduced first as it provides the framework from which action learning develops. Action learning is discussed in more detail because of its relevance to the case studies described in Chapters 4 and 5.

The concept of experiential learning is not new. It dates back to Socrates (470–399 BC) who regarded the process of becoming educated more important than arriving at some final state and with that was an advocate of life-long learning. Plato who recorded much of Socrates' thoughts suggested that any learning of which we are capable is gained by reflection on our own beliefs and is best accomplished by critical discussion with others (Crosby, 1995). In more recent times the work of Dewey (1938), Lewin (1951), Schön (1983) and Kolb (1984) has been influential in the development of experiential learning and education. As with so many other terms it is very difficult to define experiential learning (Chapman et al., 1995), however it is possible to consider the characteristics.

For Dewey (1938) the key point was that experience needed to be useable. By this he meant that experience is felt, rather than being something objective with no emotional attachment. He saw the goal of education as understanding and using experiences, which was achieved by developing thought processes with which to examine and reflect on our experiences. Experiential learning has been defined by Beard and Wilson (2002, p.16) as 'the insight gained through the conscious or unconscious internalisation of our own or observed interactions, which build upon our past experiences and knowledge'.

The most well-known experiential learning model is Kolb's (1984) experiential learning cycle. The four stages of the cycle are concrete experience, observation and reflection, abstract concepts and generalisations and then testing the learning in new situations. Whilst there are differences in terminology within other experiential learning cycles (see for example, Boud et al., 1985; Joplin, 1981), the common features are that an experience takes place – a direct first-hand learning opportunity – which is then reflected upon and the new learning and/or behaviour is then applied in a new situation, with the cycle, at that point, starting afresh.

Experiential education is a process rather than being context specific; which means it can take place anywhere at any time. In the field of management education, for example, experiential learning has taken place for a number of years, and may include, in addition to outdoor activities, the analysis of case studies, role-playing, taking part in business simulations or management games (Hussey and Lowe, 1990; Mailick and Stumpf, 1998; Mumford, 1991; Romme, 2003; Ruben, 1999). Over time these experiential approaches to management development have been added to higher education management programmes, with a number of MBA courses across the world being either completely or partly experientially based (Buller et al., 1995; Hicks, 1996; Leberman and Mellalieu, 1994; Mailick and Stumpf, 1998; McEvoy and Cragun, 1994). Given this variety, there is a need to identify some of the specific characteristics of experiential education. According to Flor (1991) these include:

- A commitment to personal growth and development of the individual through the process of group dynamics;

- An adventure component, which need not necessarily be physical, involving some degree of uncertainty and risk-taking, some challenge and reflection, a co-operative group environment and consensual decision-making, as well as a novel setting, dissonance and unique problem-solving initiatives;
- An array of 'tools of the trade' including games, initiatives and activities;
- The use of metaphors and debriefs.

The benefit of non-physical risk-taking in experiential education programmes is supported by Robinson (1992), Wagner and Campbell (1994) and Leberman and Martin (2002). Developing self-confidence and centring the locus of control within the student are also seen as important in the transfer literature. The work by Binder (1990), Robinson (1992) and Tziner, Haccoun and Kadish (1991) are examples of this. It is also argued that the propensity for taking risks will be transferred back to the work environment (Bank, 1994; Krouwel and Goodwill, 1994; Priest, 1995).

It is important that the learner is able to not only take risks during the programme, but is able to adapt the learning from those experiences to the work situation. Friedman's (1990) work focuses on the trainee, and amongst other things suggests that the trainee should take moderate risks. He states that 'these result in greater trainee growth and motivation than wild or conservative actions ... Trainees must identify projects that test their new skills, that have organisational benefits, and that have reasonable chances of success' (p.18). The aims of Robinson's (1992) study were to consider how the risk recreation experience compares subjectively to everyday working experience in its potential to generate psychological well-being, as well as to provide some qualitative information on transferability of benefits to other life spheres. The findings of Robinson's study suggested that there was some perceived transfer of psychological benefits including, for example, self-confidence, commitment and perseverance and self-determination. He sees most of the transfer as having been non-specific, in that they involved mainly principles and attitudes such as self-confidence, which is similar to the work of Bereiter (1995).

The key to experiential education is the reflection part – we all experience things in our daily lives, but all too often we just carry on and move on to the next thing rather than sitting back and taking stock of what just happened. The importance of reflection for learning is emphasised by a number of authors, particularly in the works edited by Boud, Keogh and Walker (1985) and Boud, Cohen and Walker (1993), and is highlighted in the model for promoting learning from experience (see Figure 1.1). Harris (1996) suggests that if experiential learning were to be combined with Schön's (1983) concept of 'reflection-in-action', a more useful approach to experiential learning would be available to educators and practitioners. For practitioners it is often impossible to simply apply theory to practice, due to the complex nature of the competencies required in everyday work situations and therefore practitioners develop their own theories once working in the field. For example, in Sarah's case study the Case Managers derive much of their practical expertise from trial and error approaches to situations. The service they provide is unique each time and requires a high level of interpersonal skill, given the variety of people and circumstances they have to deal with in their daily practice. It is often difficult to encapsulate in words exactly what a Case Manager actually does, but it can be demonstrated in practice, which may vary considerably depending on the individual Case Manager's experience. Gould (1996, p. 1) puts this very clearly when he says that 'reflective learning offers an approach to education which operates through an understanding of professional knowledge as primarily developed through practice and the systematic analysis of experience. This is sometimes referred to as a theory of experiential learning'.

Experience alone does not necessarily lead to learning, that is, to knowledge and understanding that the learner can adapt in other situations. 'Won't they ever learn?' is the familiar refrain about a person who repeatedly makes the same mistake. Such a person has the experience, but has failed to reflect on what happened and why. A number of the students in Stephanie's research described how through reflection they came to understand past experiences. They would recognise the similarity between what they were learning and what they had experienced in the past: 'Ahha. That's what that was! That's why that happened!' But the experience only became accessible as knowledge and understanding that could be used in new situations through the act of reflecting on past experience and learning from it. The research by Leberman and Martin (2004) supports this and suggests that Kolb's (1984) experiential learning cycle could be extended to include more than one stage of structured reflection to maximise the transfer of learning post-course.

Argyris (1994) argues that learning takes place in two ways – single-loop and double-loop. Single-loop learning occurs when decisions are made, by individuals or organisations, without examining their underlying values. Argyris provides the analogy of a thermostat, which adjusts the temperature without questioning why it is set at a certain level. In essence, the reflection part of Kolb's model is avoided. Double-loop learning adds in the reflection part, by taking a more questioning approach, 'not only about objective facts but also about the reasons and motives behind those facts' (Argyris, 1994, p.79).

The concept of mental models (Argyris and Schön, 1978; Senge, 1990) is also important here as it deals with people's biases and pre-conceived notions – how people see the world. These mental models, in turn, influence the way people understand the world, how they perceive new experiences, interpret those experiences and then generalise from them (Wyatt, 1997). Mental models form part of schema theory as discussed in Chapter 2. Four processes are identified by Wyatt (1997) as assisting in reflection, and encouraging people to move beyond their mental models. These include people learning to suspend judgement, identifying their assumptions, asking questions of themselves and listening with all their senses.

The paradox of organisational learning is that organisations learn through the experiences and actions of individuals. However, for the organisation as a whole to develop, more than individual learning needs to take place (Argyris and Schön, 1978). Kim (1993) applied the concepts of single- and double-loop learning to organisations, and regarded 'organisational learning as a metaphor derived from our understanding of individual learning' (1993, p. 37). In his model, the mental models became shared and the learning organisational, rather than individual. The challenge here is understanding how individual learning is transferred back to the organisation and how experiential programme designers working with organisations can facilitate this process. Wyatt (1997, p.84) suggests that 'the most important learning that an experiential program can transfer to an organisation is an understanding of the learning process that members experienced during the program'. In her case, this means the participant taking back the four processes of suspending judgement, identifying assumptions, asking questions and listening to the organisation.

The difficulty in achieving this in reality is highlighted by Argyris (1994). He provides a number of examples from organisations where employees have not asked questions of each other, even though they knew about double-loop learning and the importance of challenging mental models. The reasons he identifies for this not taking place are social and psychological. The social reason is linked to being considerate and positive with employees and not putting them on the spot, when the organisation is undergoing difficult changes. He sees this as managers not sharing the responsibility of bad news with employees. Argyris (1994) attributes the psychological reason for avoiding double-loop learning, to mental models developed early in life associated 'with emotional or threatening issues' (1994, p.80). He goes further to suggest that 'the purpose of this strategy is to avoid vulnerability, risk, embarrassment, and the appearance of incompetence' (1994, p.80).

This means that even if employees have been on a training course, which challenges their mental models and they have developed an espoused theory of action, their actual theory-in-use on return to the workplace may well be very different (Argyris, 1994; Schön, 1983). In many cases this takes place because, once back in the workplace, responsibility for solving problems is taken away from employees and allocated to management. By not giving employees the opportunity to practise what they have learned, the status quo is perpetuated. This, Argyris (1994) argues prevents true staff empowerment and organisational learning from taking place. Action learning, a process described next, seeks to bridge the gap between individual and organisational learning, by linking individual learning very closely with the organisation and is an important aspect of Sarah and Lex's research.

Action learning

Action learning is a form of experiential learning, which is most frequently used to meet the needs of people within a work environment, but has also been applied in increasingly diverse situations, including helping unemployed people set up their own support networks and within educational institutions. It is also particularly applicable to adult learners, as it takes into account their previous experience and enables them to build on what they already know and develop in the areas which are pertinent to them individually, both on a personal and professional basis. In a sense action learning provides what Harris (1996) suggests, namely, experiential learning combined with Schön's (1983) concept of the 'reflective practitioner'. Action learning also fits nicely with Boud and Walker's conceptual framework (see Figure 1.1).

Reg Revans is recognised as the founder of action learning – a term not used by him until the mid-1950s. The essence of action learning to Revans (1982, p. 25) is 'that those with responsible jobs to do, whether manager or not, learn best with and from each other when systematically brought together during the doing of those jobs'. The main characteristics of action learning for him are that:

- It is question rather than answer based;
- It can be used to solve some present problem;
- It is a social process with the development of a learning community;
- There is value in placing oneself in unfamiliar situations such as situations of ignorance, risk and confusion;
- Action is taken.

Much has since been written (Boddy, 1981; Dotlich and Noel, 1998; Inglis, 1994; McGill and Beaty, 1995; Weinstein, 1995) on action learning detailing its evolution, offering definitions and exploring its application in a wide variety of settings. It seems that there is difficulty in defining the concept of action learning as Revans himself never provided a single comprehensive statement (Mumford, 1991).

The role of action learning in higher education qualifications has been documented by a number of authors (see for example, Bourner and Frost, 1996; Leberman and Mellalieu, 1996; O'Hara et al., 1996). O'Hara et al. (1996) make a useful link between action learning and management education in terms of the expectations held by all the participants in the process. For the course participant, the expectation is a qualification and learning which will be beneficial to them once the course is finished. The organisation seeks a return on its investment in terms of improved organisational performance in specified areas. The higher education provider expects to contribute to 'creating new and better ways of developing managers, contributing to business success, awarding qualifications and guarding standards of education' (O'Hara et al., 1996, p.17). In the case of the research detailed in Chapter 4 similar expectations were made by the stakeholders – the Case Managers, the ACC in terms of improved service delivery to clients and the Department of Applied Social Sciences at Victoria University, as the course provider.

Another important characteristic is the view that action learning is a holistic approach, which focuses on the whole person, the personal and the professional development of an individual. Whilst much of the learning is done in groups – so-called sets – the learning is learner-driven and therefore based on the needs of the individual. Weinstein (1995, p.9), sees action learning as 'a process underpinned by a belief in individual potential: a way of learning from our actions (and from what happens to us and around us) by taking the time to question and reflect on this in order to gain insights and consider how to act in the future'. In addition, she considers two other elements to be important – that there is a group of people who work together on their doing and learning, and that there are regular and rigorous meetings of the group to allow space and time for this process of questioning and reflection.

She also identifies six elements, which she regards as critical for an action learning programme:

1. Small sets with regular meetings. A set is a small group of people – usually four to seven (McGill and Beaty, 1995); five to six (Weinstein, 1995); five to eight (Inglis, 1994) – who meet regularly and work together. Individual action and learning is the sets' *raison d'être*, rather than focusing on the group – unless team building is the objective of the group.
2. Observing airspace and questioning processes.
3. Project or task focus as a vehicle for learning.
4. Revisiting both action and learning with a set adviser until the set is able to work alone. The set adviser essentially is a facilitator of the process of action learning rather than necessarily being a subject expert. The aim is for the set adviser to become redundant in the medium to long term with the set becoming more and more independent, with individuals taking responsibility for their own learning.
5. A timeframe of no less than six months.
6. An emphasis on learning.

An addition to this list would be the need to contribute to programmed knowledge in the field of study of the action learning programme.

Raelin (1997, p.369) summarises the approach of action learning well when he states that 'action learning, ... , as a form of management education, elicits managerial behaviour, not student behaviour. Students derive knowledge not about management but rather about their own capacities to take action'. Overall, there seems to be general consensus in the literature regarding the outcomes of action learning. These include:

- Personal and professional development;
- Increased confidence and self-esteem;
- Increased self awareness;
- Learning to relate to, and communicate with, others more effectively;
- Increased readiness to take responsibility and initiative;
- A change in organisational behaviour;
- Development of networks.

All of these would indicate that both individual and organisational change has occurred, with the transfer of learning having taken place. To a large extent this is due to most action learning programmes being based both on- and off-site, and therefore addressing the issues raised by Analoui and others in the previous chapter with respect to the socio-cultural context. Similarly, the projects are 'real' rather than fabricated, which means participants can clearly see the links between what they are learning and doing at work.

SITUATED LEARNING

Situated learning and situated cognition approaches help in the understanding of learning and transfer of learning. These approaches link to the study of 'expertise', that is, how people move from being novices to experts in their field, whether it be as teachers, nurses, chess players, or hairdressers, and is particularly relevant to Lex's case study on Cook Islands teachers. The study of expertise draws on concepts and theories of experiential learning, problem-based learning, cognitive apprenticeships and anchored instruction, often emphasising types of knowledge and 'thinking' skills (Billet, 1994; Boud et al., 1993; Bransford and Schwartz, 1999; Dyson, 1999; Misko, 1995; Perkins, 1995).

Situated learning approaches structure learning situations around authentic activities, which reflect learning and application in everyday life, similar to action learning. Rather than separating learning and doing, as in the separation of 'knowing that' from 'knowing how', they are seen as interdependent. They are in keeping with Broudy's (1977) concept of 'knowing with'. Brown et al. (1989) give the example of the students of mathematics, who acquire algorithms and routines for examination purposes, but have no idea how to apply this knowledge to everyday problems and thus this knowledge remains inert.

Higher order thinking skills, authentic activities, communities of practice and the social nature of learning are all emphasised in situated learning approaches. Within situated learning contexts the focus is on the development of higher order thinking skills such as reflection, interpretation and critical thinking, rather than prioritising facts. Authentic learning activities such as problem-solving and carrying out everyday tasks enable the learner to experience the intended use of the knowledge and skills they are acquiring. The notion of a community of practice, discussed in Chapter 2 (see for example, Lave and Wenger, 1991), is an integral part of most situated learning approaches.

In the adult classroom, situated learning implies the creation of conditions of ambiguity and complexity that participants would experience in the real world. Anderson, Reder and Simon (1996) and Wilson (1993) believe that there are four major principles guiding situated learning:

1. Learning is grounded in the actions of everyday situations;
2. Knowledge is acquired situationally and can transfer only to similar situations;
3. Learning is a result of a social encounter;

4.   Learning exists in a social sense and there are actors, actions and situations.

Usually, in the adult learning classroom, learning occurs via dilemma activities (rather than transmitted by the instructor), content is inherent in the task, and the process facilitates the use of the skills in real life. Co-operative learning, immersion, interaction, observation, instructor scaffolding, practice, negotiation of meaning, problem solving, realism and higher order thinking are activities associated with authentic learning and hence are important components of the situated approach (Stein, 1998).

Those advocating situated learning approaches (Analoui, 1993; Billet, 1994; Lave and Wenger, 1991), argue that learning needs to occur within the domains and contexts in which it is to be later used, and that there will be little or no transfer to new and different contexts. The debate over the extent to which learning needs to be situated occurs in a variety of contexts including thinking, industry training and foundation learning (literacy, communication, and information and communication technologies (ICT)). On one side of the debate are those who would argue that teaching and learning needs to be context specific, and ideally 'on-the-job' (Billet, 1992, 1994). On the other side, authors such as Bransford and Schwartz (1999), would support situated learning approaches, while advocating for measures which minimise learning being context specific. These include exposing learners to diverse situations and problems, multiple perspectives, linking learning to different contexts, nurturing the skills of asking useful questions, and the reflection and abstraction of underpinning principles and knowledge.

The educator needs to be mindful of what happens to the knowledge and understanding a learner gains from a learning experience. Thinking of the computer analogy used previously in our discussion on information processing approaches (see Chapter 2), how knowledge is encoded and organised is hugely significant for its later accessibility, retrieval and use. If learning is to transfer to new and different contexts, then attention needs to be paid to cognitive processes. This requires the consideration of the encoding, organisation and retrieval of knowledge in the instructional design phase. If a course is structured around writing essays and the preparation for examinations, then knowledge will be encoded and stored for retrieval in composing essays, or for answering exam questions. The learner may effectively transfer the learning within the examination or essay situation, but is likely to have difficulty with transfer of the learning to a workplace situation.

Where a course is designed to prepare learners for future workplace situations, then future transfer needs to be addressed within the course. Essay and examination problems are likely to be well-structured, whereas everyday workplace problems are likely to be ill-structured. If the course prepares learners for future workplace problems, then knowledge will be encoded for use in authentic problem solving, or for use in identified situations in the future. The knowledge will be encoded, organised and retrieved for workplace problems. In a sense this is similar to the reflective processes highlighted by Boud and Walker in Figure 1.1.

COLLABORATIVE LEARNING

As already outlined, the social and support context of transfer of learning are important components related to its effectiveness. Hence, the development of teaching approaches that are social and collaborative can become a bridge to facilitating opportunities that promote transfer (Johnson and Johnson, 1998). Accordingly, there is considerable interest in the forms of instruction that promote social construction of learning. Indeed collaborative learning (the teaming together of students to facilitate learning) has 'come of age' at the tertiary level. Although collaboration, interdependence and co-operation have been utilised for decades in education, it is only in more recent times that the theory and practice have been recognised as being eminently suitable for the tertiary level (Millis and Cottell, 1998).

There are three major characteristics of collaborative learning. Firstly, it respects heterogeneity and encourages peer support; it is concerned with social learning and thirdly, it is an active constructive process. There are many variants of collaborative learning including for example, co-operative learning, problem based learning, informal small learning groups, simulations, role play, peer tutoring, with the application of ideas frequently being a key component of collaborative learning.

The collaborative learning approach draws upon a range of theoretical perspectives. Piaget's (1963) theories of cognitive development were based on the idea that when individuals interact with the environment, socio-cognitive conflict occurs that creates cognitive disequilibrium, which facilitates perspective taking and cognitive development. Socio-constructivist ideas grew from this theory and Vygotsky's (1978) socio-cultural theory emphasised the significance of knowledge being social and constructed from co-operative efforts. *Shared cognition theory* (or situated cognition) is different from the above mentioned theories in that the learning environment is the focus, rather than the cognitive processes (being independent of the environment). Both the physical and social contexts are the environment (Lave and Wenger, 1991).

Behavioural theory focuses on the role of reinforcers and punishers of learning, whilst Bandura's (1977) social learning theory emphasised the importance of imitation and modelling. However, one of the most significant theories impacting upon collaborative learning was the theory of social interdependence refined by Lewin (1951). This approach emphasised the importance of interdependence for group maintenance and goal accomplishment and one of Lewin's students, Deutsch, expanded this reasoning about social interdependence and formulated a theory of co-operation and competition (Deutsch, 1949, 1962).

Whilst most collaborative learning approaches involve group situations, individual coaching can also be seen as part of collaborative learning, as it involves a collaborative approach between the coach, the person being coached and the sponsoring organisation (Rosinski, 2003; Stern, 2004). Coaching is concerned with supporting a learner during the carrying out of a task to improve performance (Brown et al., 1989). It is highly interactive, situated and part of a scaffolding process (Marin, 2004), but may be as simple as hints and suggestions or even actual help to complete the task. Hence encouragement, diagnosis, directions and feedback are provided at critical phases of the instruction although eventually these are faded so that the learner becomes self-reliant. One of the very well known models of training that utilises coaching as a significant component was developed by Showers and Joyce (1996) for teacher professional development purposes. They discovered that peer coaching had a dramatic impact on transfer and on-the-job application. Training in theory, demonstration, practice and peer coaching resulted in an 80 per cent transfer rate, with coaching deemed the most potent force.

Co-operative learning has been one of the most discussed collaborative approaches and has been widely promoted for the tertiary setting (for example, Barkley et al., 2004; Millis and Cottell, 1998; Smith et al., 1997). The key elements of this approach have been identified as a common task or learning activity suitable for group work, co-operative behaviour, interdependence, small group learning and individual accountability (Davidson, 1994). Millis and Cottell (1998) note that it is becoming increasingly more acceptable at the university level to use this approach in conjunction with the more traditional lecture format. Some, however (for example, Bruffee, 1995), have been somewhat critical of its use in preference to other collaborative techniques because of its more teacher dominated approach. However, there is considerable evidence proving its value. Paradoxically, co-operative learning's supposed limitation is probably its value at the tertiary level. Time and efficiency are key university requirements and the more structured co-operative learning approach is able to provide this framework. Interestingly, it is more often the structural issues (for example, composition of group, group size, lack of accountability, responsibility for others, value of competitive context) that become the critical issues in co-operative learning although some process issues (for example, management and control of the groups, over use of the approach; preparation time, conflict of values, too much emphasis upon vague objectives and lower level thinking) also need careful consideration (Randall, 1999).

Matthews et al. (1995) view co-operative learning as a component part of collaborative learning, in which there is an emphasis upon facilitation of active learning, teaching and learning are shared between teacher and students, diversity is acknowledged as a contributor to the learning and there is a balance between lecturing and small group activities. They note that such approaches are efficient because they are potentially related to the development of higher order thinking, intellectual development, reflection, social and team skills, academic success and retention, as well as the appreciation of diversity. Furthermore, co-operative learning at the university level results in higher student achievement outcomes, improved interpersonal relations, interest in the subject, the development of higher level thinking skills, higher class morale and higher frequency and quality of interactions (Cooper and Mueck, 1990; Johnson et al., 1991; Mallinger, 1998; Shaw et al., 1999). Although many of the other studies in co-operative learning are at the school level there is ample evidence that it works at all levels of education (Bossert, 1988; Nastasi and Clements, 1992; Shaw et al., 1999).

Johnson and Johnson's (1993) meta-analysis data supported the worth of co-operative learning at the tertiary level and noted that it has a rich history, theory and practice, has valid and generalisable results rarely found elsewhere, impacts upon different instructional domains simultaneously, has identifiable components that make it work and creates learning opportunities that competitive and individual learning do not offer. Astin's (1993) important study also supported co-operative learning at the tertiary level – he found that student–student interaction and student–staff interaction were key determinants of student success. Co-operative learning was particularly important because the scrutiny of work by peers, highly motivated students and the interaction provided in-depth learning, and therefore is more likely to facilitate transfer.

TRANSFORMATIVE LEARNING

Another important aspect of adult learning is that of transformative learning, which is concerned with deeper and more lasting personal change (that is a paradigm shift) than other types of learning. It is often associated with the writings of Mezirow (1990, 1991, 1996, 1997). His work focuses on how adult learners see the world, question what they see and then develop, personally and professionally, through critical self-reflection, which is also an important factor in Boud and Walker's model (see Figure 1.1). There are two key concepts to his argument:

1. Meaning perspective, which is essentially a person's *Weltanschauung;* and
2. Meaning schemes, which are a person's perspectives deriving from their specific values, assumptions and beliefs. These schemes work together to generate a meaning perspective.

Mezirow (1997) stated that the meaning perspectives arise from life experiences, particularly those that invoke powerful emotional responses. Transformative change will not occur as long as the new material fits with the existing perspective. He believes that there are three mechanisms that create these meaning perspectives: experience, critical reflection and rational discourse. Experience is the foundation upon which reflection and discourse could change a world-view and thereby develop a more autonomous adult viewpoint. Boyd and Myers (1988) on the other hand believed it was an emotional, rather than rational component that was important for change and the end product was not increased autonomy, but an interdependent and compassionate adult. Regardless, however, of these differing views, the final outcome of this process is an empowered or self-actualised person, who reflects on their actions.

Links can be made here to Schön's (1983) concept of the reflective practitioner, as Mezirow (1991) considered reflection to be the defining quality of adult learning and the means of changing perspectives. Mezirow (1996) suggests that adult education is emancipatory in the sense that it encourages reflection and discussion, with the educator being more of a facilitator and maybe even becoming a collaborative learner. This development of a peer relationship, rather than a teacher–pupil relationship, links to the concept of action learning where the facilitator of the set works more on the peer relationship level.

The focus on process, as well as content and outcome, within adult learning is akin to Kolb's (1984) experiential learning cycle, particularly with respect to the often transformative nature of the knowledge that is gained. The importance of reflection within this context is emphasised by Williamson (1997), who also makes the link to Schön's (1983) work. In particular, Williamson (1997) draws attention to the differences between 'reflection-in-action' and 'reflection-on-action'. The former, he argues, takes place whilst something is happening. For example, in the situation of Sarah's research, the Case Manager will need to reflect on where the interview is going and how to deal with the situation as it arises. 'Reflection-on-action' may also take place, but at a later time and may also be influenced by other events that have taken place. What this means is that learning is not remote from the social and cultural context within which the individual operates. Indeed, past experiences and socialisation have a strong effect on how an individual reflects on experiences they have had (Boud and Walker, 1991).

In contrast, Reynolds (1998) argues that whilst the work of Schön (1983) and Kolb (1984) has been important in furthering the concept of reflection in management learning, they have only focused on the individual and see reflection mainly as an element of problem solving. Reynolds suggests that critical reflection is necessary for the emancipatory learning advocated by Mezirow (1990) and Cranton (1994) to take place. The characteristics of critical reflection include:

- Questioning the taken-for-granted assumptions of communities;
- Focusing on the social, political and historical nature of the experience;
- Considering power relations;
- Seeking emancipation (Reynolds, 1998).

The implications for management education are clearly stated by Reynolds (1998, p.188): 'Managing is not a neutral or disinterested activity. The socially intrusive nature of managing means involvement in and having effects on the lives of others and on their future and the future conditions of wider society'.

Reed and Anthony (1992), when discussing the need to professionalise British management, made similar comments. They believed that management education should be concerned with the issues confronting mangers in the real world, which included the fact that managers need to make moral and ethical decisions. These statements are very pertinent to the role of teachers, people in business and Case Managers, as they have an effect on people and therefore society in their daily practice.

Reynolds (1998) also suggests that much experiential learning is removed from the socio-political and cultural context within which the participants will find themselves on return to work and regards this as one of the reasons why critical reflection is often lacking in the programmes. To remedy this situation he advocates 'educational methods which lend themselves to a critical approach to content and process' and observes that 'action learning offers considerable scope for critical reflection depending on how it is interpreted in practice' (Reynolds, 1998, p.195).

Apart from the theoretical and conceptual issues surrounding transformative learning the literature has examined three other key dimensions: the roles of the participants (instructors and students), the course content, environment and instructional strategies and the challenges for instructors (see Table 3.2).

As highlighted in Table 3.2, the teaching and learning environment needs to be characterised by trust and care (Taylor, 1998), experienced mentoring as well as compassionate criticism (Boyd and Myers, 1988). The instructor/facilitator should model change (Cranton, 1994), foster personal development (Daloz, 1999) and be able to connect rational discourse with affective components (Taylor, 1998). Mezirow (1997) placed importance upon everyone having full information, being free from coercion, having the opportunity to assume different roles, being able to reflect, empathise and listen and being able to search for synthesis of views.

However, there are important challenges for the instructor/facilitator who adopts a transformative learning perspective. For example, Baumgartner (2001) questioned whether instructors have the right to encourage transformative learning and if so, can they create a safe learning environment which defuses the potential power dynamic between student and instructor? Boyd and Myers (1988) have also suggested that grieving by the student for the discarded old patterns may occur and assistance to accommodate the new thoughts may be required from the instructor.

Summary

This chapter has surveyed adult learning and provides a foundation for understanding the nature of the learner, the context for professional growth and quality learning strategies. We believe that it is important for adult educators to know their students – their needs, motivations and learning propensities. The work of Knowles (1975) highlighted this issue and has provided a framework for subsequent developments in the area. One concern we have, however, is that the literature on adult learning, professional development and change remains somewhat fragmented from each other and it is important that a more integrated approach be adopted. The specific strategies of experiential, action, situated, collaborative and transformative learning are approaches that intersect with these dimensions and provide a means of facilitating transfer. In particular, this discussion has emphasised the role of reflection on and in action as a key process to facilitate the transfer of learning, reinforcing the Boud and Walker model introduced in Chapter 1. It has also synthesised some of the main theories pertinent to facilitating the transfer of learning with adult learners, which is the focus of the

Table 3.2   The roles, course components and instructor challenges in transformative learning (adapted from Cooper, 2001)

three case studies which follow. Limited reference to the literature is made within the next

Roles	Course Components (content, environment, strategies)	Instructor Challenges
Instructor • Encourages reflection • Aware of body, mind and spirit in learning • Accepts own and others' beliefs • Cultivates alternate ways of learning • Trust and care environment • Develops sensitive relationships between participants • Serves as experienced reflective mentor • Helps students develop critical questioning. Student • Free to determine own reality • Ready and open for change • Those with wider experiences more likely to experience transformations • Ability to transcend past contexts of learning • Can engage in critical reflection • Can use both rational and affective mental functioning • Have sufficient maturity to deal with paradigm shifts.	• Reflection and discourse • Constructivist approaches • Inquiries into individual human conditions • Paradigms from other cultures • Guided imagery • Sensory awareness • Dance and movement • Breath work • Touch • Openness, safety and emotional support • All have full information and free from coercion • Students have equal opportunity to assume all roles • Empathy and search for synthesis of different points of view.	• Transference and counter transference • Confidentiality • Sexual attraction • Cognitive dissonance • Repressed memories emerging • Burnout • Appropriate supervision • Conflict between students • Classroom code of ethics • Inappropriate touch • Unprepared for transformative learning • Adequate transformative learning for the eager • Which beliefs exposed to transformation • The fine line between education and therapy.

three chapters, as it has been discussed in Chapters 2 and 3. The focus of the case studies is to highlight the participants' perspectives of the transfer of learning in three different contexts – case management, teacher training and distance learning. Readers who may care to explore other types of case studies should refer to Broad (2005).

References

Analoui, F. (1993). *Training and Transfer of Learning*, Avebury, Aldershot.
Anderson, J. R., Reder, L. M. and Simon, H. A. (1996) *Educational Researcher*, **25**, 5–11.
Argyris, C. (1994). *Harvard Business Review*, **72**, 77–85.
Argyris, C. and Schön, D. A. (1978). *Organisational Learning: A Theory of Action Perspective*, Addison-Wesley Publishing Company, Reading, MA.

Astin, A. (1993). *What Matters in College: Four Critical Years Revisited,* Jossey-Bass, San Francisco.

Bandura, A. (1977). *Social Learning Theory,* Prentice-Hall, Englewood Cliffs, NJ.

Bank, J. (1994). *Outdoor Development for Managers.,* Gower Publishing, Aldershot, UK.

Barkley, E., Cross, P. and Major, C. (2004). *Collaborative Learning Techniques: A Handbook for College Faculty,* Jossey-Bass, San Francisco, CA.

Baumgartner, L. M. (2001). *New Directions for Adult and Continuing Education,* **89,** 15–24.

Beard, C. and Wilson, J. P. (2002). *The Power of Experiential Learning – A Handbook for Trainers and Educators,* Kogan Page, London, UK.

Bellanca, J. (1996). *Designing Professional Development for Change. A Systematic Approach,* Hawker Brownlow, Highett, Victoria, Australia.

Bereiter, C. (1995). In *Teaching for Transfer: Fostering Generalization in Learning.* (eds, McKeough, A., Lupart, J. and Marini, A.) Lawrence Erlbaum Associates, Mahwah, NJ, pp. 21–34.

Billet, S. (1992). *Studies in Continuing Education,* **14,** 143–55.

Billet, S. (1994). *Vocational Aspects of Education,* **46,** 3–16.

Binder, C. (1990). *Training,* **September,** 49–56.

Boddy, D. (1981). *Journal of European Industrial Training,* **5,** 1–20.

Bossert, S. T. (1988). In *Review of Research in Education,* Vol. 15 (ed., Rothkopf, E. Z.) American Educational Research Association, Washington, DC, pp. 225–50.

Boud, D., Cohen, R. and Walker, D. (eds) (1993). *Using Experience for Learning,* Open University Press, Buckingham.

Boud, D. and Griffin, V. (1987). *Appreciating Adults Learning: From the Learner's Perspective,* Kogan Page, London.

Boud, D., Keogh, R. and Walker, D. (eds) (1985). *Reflection: Turning Experience into Learning,* Kogan Page, London.

Boud, D. and Walker, D. (1991) *Experience and Learning: Reflection at Work,* Deakin University Press, Geelong.

Bourner, T. and Frost, P. (1996). *Education & Training,* **38,** 22–31.

Boyd, R. D. and Myers, J. G. (1988). *International Journal of Lifelong Education,* **7,** 261–84.

Brandes, D. and Ginnes, P. (1986). *A Guide to Student-centred Learning,* Blackwell, Oxford, UK.

Bransford, J. D. and Schwartz, D. L. (1999). *Review of Research in Education,* **24,** 61–100.

Broad, M. L. (2005). *Beyond Transfer of Training: Engaging Systems to Improve Performance,* Pfeiffer, San Francisco, CA.

Brookfield, S. D. (1986). *Understanding and Facilitating Adult Learning,* Jossey-Bass, San Francisco, CA.

Broudy, H. S. (1977). In *Schooling and the Acquisition of Knowledge.* (eds, Anderson, R. C., Spiro, R. J. and Montague, W. E.) Lawrence Earlbaum Associates, Hillsdale, NJ, pp. 1–17.

Brown, J. S., Collins, A. and Duguid, P. (1989). *Educational Researcher,* **18,** 32–42.

Bruffee, K. (1995). *Collaborative Learning: Higher Education, Interdependence, and the Authority of Knowledge,* John Hopkins University Press, Baltimore, MD.

Brundage, D. and MacKeracher, D. (1980). *Adult Learning Principles and Their Application to Program Planning,* Ministry of Education, Toronto.

Buller, P. F., McEvoy, G. M. and Cragun, J. R. (1995). *Journal of Management Education,* **19,** 35–53.

Castaldi, T. M. (1989). *Lifelong Learning,* **12,** 17–19.

Chapman, S., McPhee, P. and Proudman, B. (1995). In *The Theory of Experiential Education.* (eds, Warren, K., Sakofs, M. and Hunt, J. S. J.) Kendall/Hunt Publishing Company, Dubuque, IO, pp. 235–48.

Cheetham, G. and Chivers, G. (1996). *Journal of European Industrial Training,* **20,** 20–30.

Cheetham, G. and Chivers, G. (2000). In *41st Adult Education Research Conference.* (eds, Sork, T. J., Chapman, V. and St Clair, R.) University of British Columbia, Vancouver, Canada, pp. 549–50.

Cooper, S. (2001). *Transformational Learning.* Retrieved 20 June, 2005, from www.konnections.net/lifecircles/translearn.htm

Cooper, J. and Mueck, R. (1990). *Excellence in College Teaching,* **1,** 68–76.

Cranton, P. (1994). *Understanding and Promoting Transformative Learning: A Guide for Educators of Adults,* Jossey-Bass, San Francisco, CA.

Crosby, A. (1995). In *The Theory of Experiential Education.* (eds, Warren, K., Sakofs, M. and Hunt, J. S. J.) Kendall/Hunt Publishing Company, Dubuque, IO, pp. 3–14.

Cross, K. P. (1981). *Adults as Learners,* Jossey-Bass, San Francisco, CA.

Daloz, L. A. (1999). *Mentor: Guiding the Journey of Adult Learners,* Jossey-Bass, San Francisco, CA.

Davidson, N. (1994). In *Creativity and Collaborative Learning: A Practical Guide to Empowering Students and Teachers.* (eds, Thousand, J. S., Villa, R. A. and Nevin, A. I.) Paul H. Brookes Publishing Co., Baltimore, MD, pp. 13–30.

Deutsch, M. (1949). *Human Relations,* **2,** 199–231.

Deutsch, M. (1962). In *Nebraska Symposium on Motivation.* (ed., Jones, M. R.) University of Nebraska, Lincoln, NB, pp. 275–320.

Dewey, J. (1938). *Experience and Education,* Collier, New York.

Dotlich, D. L. and Noel, J. L. (1998). *Action Learning: How the World's Top Companies are Re-creating Their Leaders and Themselves.,* Jossey-Bass, San Francisco, CA.

Dreyfus, H. L. and Dreyfus, S. E. (1986). *Mind Over Machine: The Power of Human Intuition and Expertise in the Era of the Computer,* The Free Press, New York.

Dyson, A. H. (1999). *Review of Research in Education,* **24,** 141–71.

Ellsworth, J. B. (2000). ERIC Clearinghouse on Information and Technology, Syracuse University, New York.

Ely, D. (1990). *Journal of Research on Computing in Education,* **23,** 298–305.

Eraut, M. (1994). *Developing Professional Knowledge and Competence,* Falmer Press, London.

Ferguson, M. (1980). In *Theories and models in applied behavioural science.* (eds. Pfeiffer, J. W. and Ballew, A. C.) Pfeiffer & Co., San Diego, CA, pp. 223-225.

Flor, R. (1991). *Journal of Experiential Education,* **14,** 27–34.

Friedman, B. A. (1990). *Training & Development Journal,* **December,** 17–19.

Freiere, P. (1970). *Pedagogy of the Oppressed,* Penguin, London.

Ford, J. K. (1994). Defining transfer of learning. The meaning is in the answers. *Adult learning,* **5,** 22-24.

Fullan, M. G. (1991). *The New Meaning of Educational Change,* Cassell, London.

Gould, N. (1996). In *Reflective Learning for Social Work: Research, Theory and Practice.* (eds, Gould, N. and Taylor, I.) Arena Ashgate Publishing Limited, Aldershot, pp. 1–10.

Hall, G. E. and Hord, S. E. (1987). *Change in Schools: Facilitating the Process,* State University of New York, Albany, NY.

Harris, A. (1996). In *Reflective Learning for Social Work: Research, Theory and Practice.* (eds, Gould, N. and Taylor, I.) Arena Ashgate Publishing Limited, Aldershot, pp. 35–46.

Haskell, R. E. (2001). *Transfer of Learning: Cognition, Instruction and Reasoning.* Academic Press, San Diego, CA.

Havelock, R. and Zlotolow, S. (1995). *The Change Agent's Guide,* Educational Technology Publications, Englewood Cliffs, NJ.

Hicks, R. E. (1996). *Education & Training,* **38,** 28–38.

Hussey, D. and Lowe, P. (eds) (1990). *Key Issues in Management Training,* Kogan Page, London, UK.

Imel, S. (1995). ERIC Clearing House on Adult, Career and Vocational Education, Centre on Education and Training for Employment, Ohio State University, Columbus, OH.

Imel, S. (2000). ERIC Clearing House on Adult, Career and Vocational Education, Centre on Education and Training for Employment, The Ohio State University, Columbus, OH.

Inglis, S. (1994). *Making the Most of Action Learning,* Gower, Aldershot.

Johnson, D. and Johnson, R. (1993). *Cooperative Learning and College Teaching,* **3,** 6–9.

Johnson, D. and Johnson, R. (1998). *Social Psychological Applications to Social Issues. Cooperatuve Learning and Social Interdependence Theory.* Retrieved 12 August 2001, from http://www.clerc.com/pages/SIT. html

Johnson, D. W., Johnson, R. T. and Smith, K. (1991). George Washington University, Washington DC.

Joplin, L. (1981). *The Journal of Experiential Education,* **4,** 17–20.

Kim, D. H. (1993). *Sloan Management Review,* **35,** 37–50.

Knowles, M. (1975). *Self-directed Learning,* Follet, Chicago.

Knowles, M. (1980). *The Modern Practice of Adult Education,* Follet, Chicago, IL.

Knowles, M. (1984a). *The Adult Learner: A Neglected Species,* Gulf Publishing, Houston, TX.

Knowles, M. (1984b). *Andragogy in Action,* Jossey-Bass, San Francisco, CA.

Knowles, M. and Associates (eds) (1985). *Andragogy in Action: Applying Modern Principles of Adult Learning,* Jossey-Bass, San Francisco.

Knowles, M. S., Holton, E. F. I. and Swanson, R. A. (2005). *The Adult Learner,* Elsevier, Boston, MA.

Knox, A. B. (1986). *Helping Adults Learn,* Jossey-Bass, San Francisco, CA.

Kolb, D. A. (1984). *Experiential Learning: Experience as the Source of Learning and Development,* Prentice-Hall, New York.

Krouwel, B. and Goodwill, S. (1994). *Management Development Outdoors: A Practical Guide to Getting the Best Results,* Kogan Page, London.

Lave, J. and Wenger, E. (1991). *Situated Learning: Legitimate Peripheral Participation,* Cambridge University Press, Cambridge.

Leberman, S. I. and Martin, A. J. (2002). *Australian Journal of Outdoor Education,* **7,** 71–81.

Leberman, S. I. and Martin, A. J. (2004). *Journal of Adventure Education & Outdoor Learning*, **4**, 173–84.

Leberman, S. I. and Mellalieu, P. J. (1994). In *3rd International Organisational Behaviour Teaching Conference*. (ed., Stablein, R.) University of Otago, Dunedin, New Zealand, pp. 61–2.

Leberman, S. I. and Mellalieu, P. J. (1996). In *From Mystery to Mastery – Mai I Te Ao Ngaro Ki Te Ao Marama. Outdoor Education Conference*. Sir Edmund Hillary Outdoor Pursuits Centre of New Zealand, Turangi, New Zealand, pp. 1–15.

Lewin, K. (1951). *Field Theory in Social Sciences*, Harper and Row, New York.

Lippit, R., Watson, J. and Westley, B. (1958). *The Dynamics of Planned Change*, Harcourt, Brace and World, New York.

Mailick, S. and Stumpf, S. A. (1998). *Learning Theory in the Practice of Management Development: Evolution and Applications*, Quorum Books, Westport, CT.

Mallinger, M. (1998). *Journal of Management Education*, **22**, 472–583.

Marin, R. (2004). *Modelling, Coaching and Scaffolding*. Retrieved 12 January 2006, from http://coe.sdsu.edu/eet/articles/learnstrategy/start/htm

Matthews, R. S., Cooper, J. L., Davidson, N. and Hawkes, P. (1995). In *Change: The Magazine of Higher Learning*, Vol. July/August, pp. 34–9.

McDonald, B. L. (2002). In *Department of Education*, Victoria University of Wellington, Wellington, New Zealand.

McDonald, B. L. (2005). In *New Zealand Annual Review of Education 14: 2004* (ed., Livingston, I.) School of Educational Studies, Victoria University of Wellington, Wellington, New Zealand, pp. 21–38.

McEvoy, G. and Cragun, J. (1994). In *3rd International Organisational Behaviour Teaching Conference*. (ed., Stablein, R.) University of Otago, Dunedin, New Zealand, pp. 24–6.

McGill, I. and Beaty, L. (1995). *Action Learning: A Guide for Professional Development, Management and Educational Development.*, Kogan Page, London.

Merriam, S. B. and Caffarella, R. (1998). *Learning in Adulthood*, Jossey-Bass, New York.

Mezirow, J. (1981). *Adult Education*, **32**, 3–27.

Mezirow, J. (1991). *Transformative Dimensions of Adult Learning*, Jossey-Bass, San Francisco, CA.

Mezirow, J. (1996). *Adult Education Quarterly*, **46**, 158–73.

Mezirow, J. (1997). *New Directions for Adult and Continuing Education*, **74**, 5–12.

Mezirow, J. and Associates (1990). *Fostering Critical Reflection in Adulthood: A Guide to Transformative and Emancipatory Learning*, Jossey-Bass, San Francisco, CA.

Millis, B. J. and Cottell, P. G. J. (1998). *Cooperative Learning for Higher Education Faculty*, American Council on Education, Oryx Press, Phoenix, AZ.

Misko, J. (1995). *Transfer: Using Learning in New Contexts*, National Council for Vocational Educational Research, Adelaide, Australia.

Mumford, A. (ed.) (1991). *Gower Handbook of Management Development*, Gower Publishing Company Limited, Aldershot, UK.

Nastasi, B. K. and Clements, D. H. (1992). *Learning and Instruction*, **2**, 215–38.

O'Hara, S., Webber, T. and Reeve, S. (1996). *Education & Training*, **38**, 16–21.

Organisation for Economic Co-operation and Development (1998). *Staying Ahead. Inservice Training and Teacher Professional Development*. Centre for Educational Research and Innovation, OECD, Paris.

Perkins, D. N. (1995). *Outsmarting IQ: The Emerging Science of Learnable Intelligence*, The Free Press, New York.

Piaget, J. (1963). *The Origins of Intelligence in Children*, Northern, New York.

Priest, S. J. (1995). *Corporate Adventure Training in a Suspicious Marketplace!* (Unpublished Paper). Sir Edmund Hillary Outdoor Pursuits Centre: Turangi.

Raelin, J. A. (1997). *Journal of Management Education*, **21**, 368–94.

Randall, V. (1999). *The Education Digest*, **65**, 29–32.

Reed, M. and Anthony, P. (1992). *Journal of Management Studies*, **29**, 591–613.

Reigeluth, C. and Garfinkle, R. (1994). *Systemic Change in Education*, Educational Technology Publications, Englewood Cliffs, NJ.

Revans, R. W. (1982). *Journal of Management Development*, **3**, 15–26.

Reynolds, M. (1998). *Management Learning*, **29**, 183–200.

Robinson, D. W. (1992). *Journal of Applied Recreation Research*, **1**, 12–36.

Rogers, E. M. (1995). *Diffusion of Innovations*, The Free Press, New York.

Romme, A. G. L. (2003). *Management Learning*, **34**, 51–61.

Rosinski, P. (2003). *Coaching Across Cultures*, Nicholas Brealey, London.

Ruben, B. D. (1999). *Simulation & Gaming*, **30**, 498–505.

Schön, D. A. (1983). *The Reflective Practitioner: How Professionals Think in Action*, Basic Books Inc., New

York.

Senge, P. M. (1990). *The Fifth Discipline: The Art and Practice of the Learning Organisation,* Double Day, New York.

Shaw, J. B., Fisher, C. D. and Southey, G. N. (1999). *Journal of Management Development,* **23,** 509–36.

Showers, B. and Joyce, B. (1996). *Educational Leadership,* **53,** 12–16.

Smith, E., Ford, J. K. and Kozlowski, S. W. J. (1997). In *Training for a Rapidly Changing Workplace: Applications of Psychological Research.* (eds, Quinones, M. A. and Ehrenstein, A.) American Psychological Association, Washington DC, pp. 89–118.

St Clair, R. (2002). In *ERIC Myths and Realities,* ERIC Clearing House on Adult, Career and Vocational Education, Columbus, OH.

Stein, D. (1998). *Situated Learning in Adult Education,* ERIC Clearing House on Elementary and Early Childhood Education ED 418250, Urbana, IL.

Stern, L. R. (2004). *Consulting Psychology Journal: Practice and Research,* **56,** 154–62.

Surry, D., Porter, B., Jackson, K. and Hall, D. (2004). Vol. 2005 Atlanta, GA, pp. Proceedings of the Society for Information Technology and Teacher Education International Conference.

Taylor, E. W. (1998). *The Theory and Practice of Transformational Learning: A Critical Review,* ERIC Clearing House on Adult, Career, & Vocational Education, Columbus, OH.

Tziner, A., Haccoun, R. R. and Kadish, A. (1991). *Journal of Occupational Psychology,* **64,** 167–77.

Vygotsky, L. S. (1978). *Mind in Society.* Harvard University Press, Cambridge, MA.

Wagner, R. J., and Campbell, J. (1994). Outdoor-based Experiential Training: Improving Transfer Using Virtual Reality. *Journal of Management Development,* **13,** 4-11.

Weinstein, K. (1995). *Action Learning: A Journey in Discovery and Development,* Harper Collins Publishers, London.

Williamson, A. (1997). *Australian Journal of Adult and Community Education,* **37,** 93–9.

Wilson, A. (1993). In *An Update on Adult Learning Theory* (ed., Merriam, S. B.) Jossey-Bass, San Francisco, pp. 71–9.

Wlodkowski, R. J. (2003). *New Directions for Adult and Continuing Education,* **98,** 39–47.

Wyatt, S. (1997). *Journal of Experiential Education,* **20,** 80–5.

Zaltman, G. and Duncan, R. (1977). *Strategies for Planned Change,* John Wiley and Sons, New York.

4 *Transfer of Learning from the Classroom to the Workplace: A Longitudinal Case Study with Case Managers*

This chapter summarises Sarah Leberman's research into the transfer of learning of the Accident Rehabilitation and Compensation Insurance Corporation (ACC) Case Managers from the classroom to the workplace (Leberman, 1999). The research took place between 1996 and 1999. Her complete thesis is available online in PDF format at www.massey.ac.nz/~sleberma/

Context and overview

The transfer of learning is seen as an important part of any course of study. This is of particular importance when employers are paying for their staff to attend the courses. How do they know whether they receive a return on their investment? How long before the course fades into insignificance? What are the key components, which facilitate this transfer of learning?

In the context of this research particular interest was on the long-term effect training had once back in the workplace (up to two years post-training), how to avoid the 'fade-out' effect and the identification of factors which facilitate transfer. The focus was on the management of the transfer process as it applied to service management, and in particular case management services delivered by ACC.

The purpose of the research was to identify the factors, which facilitated the transfer of learning from an adult learning environment, using action learning methods of instruction, to the workplace. The research also sought to develop a model which optimises the transfer of learning from the classroom to the workplace for adult learners.

This research focused on the transfer of learning from the classroom to the workplace of Case Managers, who were working for the ACC during the period 1995 to 1998. The 47 participants in this research were graduates of the first three cohorts of students from the Victoria University of Wellington (VUW) Diploma in Rehabilitation Studies. The longitudinal case study adopted for this research was set within a phenomenological paradigm, with the methodology being informed by grounded research. The methods of data collection included semi-structured and unstructured, face-to-face and telephone interviews, as well as focus groups. The data collection took place at six-monthly intervals post-course – at 12 months, 18 months and 24 months. By the third time interval the number of research participants had diminished to 38.

THE ACC AND CASE MANAGEMENT

The ACC is a government agency, which provides for no-fault, rehabilitation and compensation insurance 24 hours a day to all New Zealanders. The principles and parameters of ACC operations are set out in the ARCIC Act 1992, which describes the main areas of activity as injury prevention, rehabilitation and compensation. The ACC scheme was based on the notion that 'the people of New Zealand should share responsibility for the consequences of accidental injury, regardless of cause or fault, and that the injured should be effectively treated, and returned to their role in the community as quickly as possible, without significant personal financial loss' (Accident Rehabilitation and Compensation Insurance Company, 1995, p. 5).

The aim of case management was to provide a high quality outcome focused service, resulting in a faster and better recovery for claimants and ultimately a reduction in duration and costs of claims. Case management was introduced overnight with many clerical workers instantly becoming Case Managers. No training in case management was provided to staff prior to implementation and the subsequent two-day Platform training offered was essentially content driven. By the end of 1994 the ACC realised that there was a need for more in-depth training.

THE VUW DIPLOMA IN REHABILITATION STUDIES

In December of 1994, Victoria University of Wellington was approached by the ACC to design and deliver a tailor-made course, which would change the practice of their Case Managers and improve service delivery through case management. The course was fully funded by the ACC and consisted of the 27-week post-experience VUW Diploma in Rehabilitation Studies. The VUW Diploma was divided into a 12-week residential period at Victoria University covering six modules of study, followed by a supervised 14-week work-based practicum – module seven, which included conducting a Case Study with a client and a research project. The eighth and final module was held back in Wellington

The first part involved seven one-week modules completed over the course of 12 weeks, with directed study and group work tasks built into each alternative week when students completed assignments and explored how the learning from each module might be applied back to the workplace. These study weeks were seen as integral to the concept of developing reflective practitioners, in that they enabled students to reflect on the content of the preceding module and how it applied to their work situation. This built on the notion that often more is learned when less content is covered (Maier, 1994). The students were required to keep a journal throughout the 27 weeks, which encouraged them to develop the habit of reflecting on their daily experiences, rather than merely 'doing' or 'participating' in activities and classes.

A supervised 14-week practicum followed the 12-week modular part of the VUW Diploma. During the practicum the students fulfilled the requirements of their individual learning contract, carried out a practice study, undertook a taped interview and completed their rehabilitation project. Throughout the practicum the students were expected to carry out their normal duties as Case Managers, so as to practise and apply their newly found skills and knowledge.

The six critical elements for an action learning programme (see Chapter 3) identified by Weinstein were present during the students' time in Wellington and whilst on practicum back at their branches. The sets were the four regional groups and the set adviser the regional tutor, with the group becoming essentially autonomous by the time they left Wellington. Whilst the students were not necessarily physically in one place, support networks were set up via email and telephone, as well as regional get-togethers. There were a number of mini projects leading up to the main project completed during their time back in the branch. This main research project has led to a substantial increase in the programmed knowledge associated with the ACC and rehabilitation issues.

Findings

The findings suggest that the key factor facilitating the transfer of learning from the classroom to the workplace for adult learners is the use of a course design that employs experiential/action learning, which incorporates both personal and professional development modules, as well as a work-based practicum. This is well summarised by the following participant responses:

It was good, excellent – I would never have coped with full-on study. The combination of personal and professional worked well because the personal part is so important in the role of rehabilitation. You have to be a part of people's lives, but must also be able to stand back … It's really important that there is a mix, as there is no set way to do rehabilitation because everyone is different.

The Victoria course makes an ordinary person a Case Manager. I had the skills to be doing administration and basic skills to interview people. The course said forget about entitlements and legislation and find out what the person needs and then work out how to manage the situation within the confines we have.

The emphasis needs to be on student-centred learning, which enables participants to reflect on and learn from their personal and professional experiences. At the same time it encourages the participants to push the boundary of their 'comfort zone', which facilitates personal development. The importance of personal development for people working in the human services should not be underestimated, particularly for customer-contact workers.

In the case of this research, it was shown that confident and more self-aware Case Managers were able to provide a better service to their clients, than was the case prior to having completed the VUW Diploma in Rehabilitation Studies. Participants highlighted these points as follows:

I now have the confidence to stick up for what I believe is right.

Pre-course I would have steered clear of attempted sexual abuse victim clients, but now I am confident and able to talk with other professionals including lawyers and doctors.

Pre-course I wasn't confident negotiating with employers. The course gave me the confidence to successfully negotiate return-to-work trials. I can now see through all the game-playing authoritarian type employers. To have this is a major achievement.

Marae stay had most effect on me personally. It developed my self-awareness and that of other people. It made me think a lot about me, where I am at, where I am going and gave me a definition of cultural safety, which was that I needed to know who I was first – not what Maori had for breakfast.

The participants' perceptions of being able to provide an improved service to their clients as a result of the training they received, was important and provided an insight into why improved service delivery took place.

What you do on the course becomes part of your everyday life and is still very valuable.

The course is still useful, as I often think of it when I do things and realise that I did them like that because of the course.

Things like conflict resolution and needs assessment have now become second nature. If I had to sit down and break down what I do that has come from the course it would be hard to do.

The course still has a huge relevance to what I'm doing now. Listening skills and looking at rehab plans. Things come to me everyday and I don't even think about it. Things like stress management, negotiation skills, time management and other little things I do that remind me of the course. Having done the course affects my own work practice. It's sometimes hard to filter out what you're using and what you're not. The course has changed my whole way of thinking with respect to rehab – what I do now just happens.

However, managers need to know that this is actually happening. For the ACC this could be determined by an analysis of the number of cases handled, the percentage of claimants no longer funded by ACC or the amount of money saved by each Case Manager. These data were not specifically collected as part of this research, as the focus was on the experiences of the participants, even though many participants volunteered such data. The other option would have been to conduct a customer service questionnaire to ascertain the level of client satisfaction.

Some of the qualitative data collected in this study offered tangible indicators of improved service delivery, particularly with respect to reducing the number of claimants financially supported by the ACC and therefore saving the organisation money. The following comments illustrate this claim.

On average I've got off two of my +52 week claimants per month ... all from the skills learned on the course.

My +52 week load has reduced by over 50% in the last 12 months because of my initial assessments.

I've had the third most closures in the branch.

The two of us working with the long-term claimants have got 60 out of 80 off the scheme.

I've saved ACC $300 000 and it could be more if I had the time.

I've got 40 people back to work since August so I'm nearly at the $2 million savings mark.

The number of participants who were either promoted, worked with serious and complex injury cases or selected to work on a special project: Rehabilitation and Review of Long-Term Claimants (RARLTC), suggested that the ACC valued their skills and knowledge. Overall 29 participants were involved. Five participants were promoted to Head Office and ten to more senior positions in either their Branch or region. Seven participants were selected to work on the serious and more complex injury files, with one participant stating that 'the more complex cases are given to Case Managers who've been through the course, although this may depend on the branch'. A further seven participants focused on RARLTC, which one participant directly attributed to the VUW Diploma in Rehabilitation Studies by saying 'I was picked to do this because I'd done the course'.

These research findings were supported by the Collinson and Brook (1997) study, which reported how both the participants and supervisors indicated that the VUW Diploma in Rehabilitation Studies had led to improved claimant management due to a more professional approach and that this was associated with a subsequent reduction in costs to the ACC. Collinson and Brook also highlighted how the participants had become role models for their colleagues, as well as being sources of information and advice. This may have had a positive effect on the service delivered by all employees, rather than only those who participated on the course.

Most organisations tend to focus their training activities on professional development and on specific skills required for the job, but neglect to develop the person at the same time. This research indicated that once personal development has taken place, people are able to make use of job specific skills learned during training to provide, in this case, a better case management service to clients. In addition, the combination of personal and professional development had led to a change in personal case management practice. This signalled a more long-term benefit to the organisation as for many participants, their new way of being and working had become second nature.

The combination of off- and on-site training also appeared to have been important. The use of a work-based practicum, following the University-based modules, enabled participants to transition back to the workplace in a gradual manner. During this time they were able to readjust to both the home and work environments, whilst still working on specific personalised learning objectives. These learning objectives, together with the Case Study and the Research Project provided specific opportunities for using newly acquired skills and knowledge. It meant that participants were not 'dropped' straight back into their workplace without provision for testing what they had learned.

The role the ACC played in facilitating the transfer of learning remains unclear. The findings implied that the desired organisational outcome of improved case management service was achieved in spite of numerous organisational detractions, which occurred during the research period, illustrated by the following participant observations:

People in the branch labelled you as tall poppies – it would have been better if they'd had nothing to compare you to.

It was hard during the practicum due to the lack of support from fellow staff members.

On return from the course there was an anti-feeling to the course, but that has changed now that more people have been through the course. There are also more professionals in the branch so I don't stand out as much any more.

The branch climate has not let us be change agents – not to the extent we had been encouraged to. On return I tried to encourage staff to focus on getting out rather than processing – but it wasn't realistic. My approach is now more client focused and I try to convey this to other staff. There has been little opportunity to change the organisation. Too few resources to achieve things.

It was very difficult settling again on return to the Branch, it took a long time assimilating back into the Branch; maybe my expectations were a little high – it was and is very frustrating as I can't do what I want to do. I have saved ACC $300,000 whilst still doing mainly processing but focusing on vocational rehabilitation. If I had the time to do the real stuff it could be a million.

The service management and transfer literature, as well as common sense, would suggest that transfer will be more successful if the whole organisation is supportive of the training. This means that training needs to be an integral component of the organisation's service management strategy. In this case, it may be that people were better at riding the waves of change as a result of training that incorporated both personal and professional development. Constant change does not present opportunities to become complacent; instead the expectation is that people will rise to the challenges as they occur. There were, however, a number of participants who either chose to leave the organisation, or were actively looking for new employment because of the unsupportive nature of the ACC and the constant changes they were experiencing. As a consequence the ACC lost a number of valuable Case Managers, which impacted not only on their service delivery, but also provided little return to the organisation in terms of money and time invested in supporting staff through professional training. On balance, an organisation needs to provide more support than detractions in order to achieve higher levels of transfer of learning.

Collinson and Brook (1997) also drew attention to ways in which organisational support was limited. Both participants and supervisors commented on this aspect. The supervisors indicated that contributing factors included limited resources, legislative restrictions, too little time and high case-loads.

A GENERIC TRANSFER OF LEARNING MODEL

The conclusions from the research have been incorporated into a generic transfer of learning model which, it is suggested, explains the preferred conditions for transfer of learning from the classroom to the workplace for adult learners, illustrated in Figure 4.1. The model identifies three building blocks that are necessary for the transfer of learning to take place. These are: Educational Process, Personal Development and Job Specific Processes. The Educational Process is the foundation upon which everything else builds. The Educational Process encourages the personal and skill development of individual participants, which empowers participants to employ the Job Specific Processes needed to achieve desired outcomes. The fluidity and interaction between the three building blocks is represented by the dotted lines. The importance of organisational support has been discussed above. Organisational Support is, therefore, shown as larger than Organisational Detractions in Figure 4.1 because it is unrealistic to suggest there will be no detractions, particularly if this model is to be applicable to both government and private organisations.

This model contributes to the existing knowledge in the transfer of training/learning field as found in the service management and transfer literature (Analoui, 1993; Broad and Newstrom, 1992; Gregoire et al., 1998; Holton, 1996). It integrates elements pertinent to this research into a wider theoretical model. The model was derived from the experiences of course participants and focuses on the educational process, whereas existing models have been based on training provider and organisational perceptions, as well as reviews of the literature. The importance of the teaching methodology and the selection of appropriate learning activities

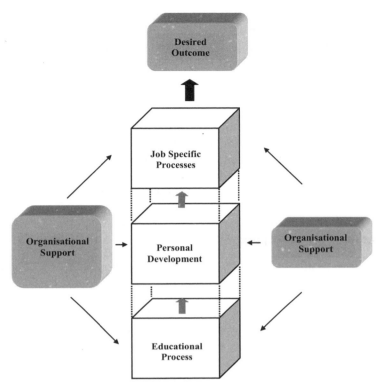

Figure 4.1   Recommended transfer of learning model (Leberman, 1999, p.223)

has been highlighted in the literature (Analoui, 1993; Gass, 1989; McGraw, 1993). This model therefore endorses these observations from the participant's perspective.

It is recognised that the elements of the Transfer of Learning Model suggested in Figure 4.1 do not interact in a vacuum, but are influenced by the social, cultural, economic and political environments, within which they operate. Depending on the situation, these environments may have a supportive or detracting influence on the various elements of the model. The extent of generalisation from the research is limited, but is concordant with the nature of qualitative research, which seeks to form unique interpretations of events rather than produce generalisations (Seng, 1998). The credibility and dependability of the research was enhanced by triangulating the data between the three cohorts (Denzin and Lincoln, 1994; Yin, 1994).

Implications for management

TRAINING AND STRATEGIC GOALS

Management must consider how training and development programmes link into the overall strategic goals of the organisation. For maximum benefit, the training and development programmes should be aligned with the organisation's strategic directions. This may pose difficulties for large government service organisations like the ACC because of the constant changes in policies and/or government, to which they are subjected. It is important for the organisation to clearly identify the desired learning outcomes and then ensure that the organisation provides opportunities to implement the learning. In this research the target organisation's approach to case management changed part-way through the research process. The original learning outcomes specified being able to adopt an holistic approach to case management so as to improve service delivery to ACC claimants. However, this emphasis on using an holistic approach changed with the formation of a new government in October 1996. The focus throughout 1997 became that of saving money, a focus that was further emphasised with the appointment of a new CEO at the end of 1997. The aim was to reduce the number of long-term claimants as fast as possible, and not to look at each situation in an holistic manner. This complete change in emphasis resulted in many of the participants being compromised. They had been sent on a course to learn a certain approach, which they did. However, on return to their branch they were not encouraged to use this approach and found themselves in difficult situations.

ADOPTING AN INCLUSIVE APPROACH

All levels of the organisation affected by training and development programmes should be involved in the planning stages. This will ensure that both participants and non-participants are aware of the programmes, what they aim to achieve and how the training process may affect the workplace. This is especially pertinent to immediate colleagues and their supervisors. The findings suggested that the ACC was not particularly successful in communicating the educational process of the VUW Diploma in Rehabilitation Studies, the associated expectations placed on the Principle Case Managers and the workplace implications of the practicum. In order to facilitate the transfer of learning, organisations need to ensure that the appropriate structures and procedures are in place for participants to be supported throughout the training process. This is particularly important for large national service organisations, which may have a centralised Head Office with local branches delivering services to the community.

RECOGNITION OF TRAINING AND POSSIBILITIES FOR ADVANCEMENT

Management needs to ensure that successful completion of training is recognised in performance appraisals and where appropriate rewarded in financial terms. It is also important to provide opportunities for training participants to extend themselves or progress in their careers on return to the workplace. Failure to do so may result in skilled employees leaving the organisation. This represents not only a skill and knowledge loss, but also a financial loss in terms of the training time and money invested. Five participants in this research left the ACC for these very reasons. A number of other participants were actively seeking new positions outside the organisation, as they felt that their work was not recognised and there was a lack of opportunities for professional advancement. Staff needs to be valued as a scarce resource and as real people who have a contribution to make. Training and development programmes which focus on both personal and professional development are more likely to have long-term effects, particularly when specific skills required of employees may change in a short period of time. If employees are self-confident independent thinkers with a desire to learn, the change process may be much easier to achieve, and new skills or processes more readily adopted.

Implications for professional practice

THE TIME SPENT PLANNING WILL PAY OFF IN THE LONG RUN

Before developing training opportunities for staff it is important to clearly identify the desired outcome(s) of the training. This process should involve all the key stakeholders, including potential course participants and supervisors. Once this has been established, a training provider should be contracted who is able to work with the organisation to develop a tailor-made training programme. Time needs to be set aside for planning not only the course content in conjunction with the training provider, but also for ensuring operational details are organised, including transport, accommodation and cover for staff attending the training. These operational factors may appear trivial, but experience with the VUW Diploma in Rehabilitation Studies would suggest that students struggle to focus on the training when these primary needs are not met. It is also important to review each training opportunity involving the organisation, the training provider and the participants, so that improvements can be made to future training.

TRAINING COURSES NEED TO BE APPROPRIATE TO THE PARTICIPANTS

When designing training courses it is important to consider carefully who the participants are going to be, as well as having an appreciation of their backgrounds. In general, there are a number of ways in which desired outcomes can be achieved, with the process used varying depending on the situation. This is where tailor-made training courses come to the fore. Delivering training courses to adult learners generally means that the participants come from a heterogeneous background, bringing with them a range of preferred learning styles and a myriad of experiences on which they can draw. It is, therefore, important that the educational process adopted is flexible enough to cater to the diverse needs of the participants, so that they all have the opportunity to develop, both personally and professionally, through the training.

THE IMPORTANCE OF EXPERIENTIAL/ACTION LEARNING APPROACHES WITH ADULT LEARNERS IS NOT TO BE UNDERESTIMATED

The experiential/action learning approach offers a process, which is flexible in terms of design and provides the capacity to meet the differing needs of different learners. The focus on action and reflection, as well as personal and professional development, provides a variety of learning opportunities for participants. Experiential learning encompasses numerous delivery options including indoor and outdoor, physical and non-physical. The key point to note is that the choice of delivery option needs to be suited to the participants and enable the desired outcome(s) to be achieved. Taking a group of people on a three-day outdoor management development programme may not be the best option for the participants, nor will it necessarily achieve the desired outcome(s). The action learning approach falls within the options offered in experiential learning. It provides a specific tie-in with the organisation in terms of using work-based projects as the basis for personal and professional development, as well as using learning sets where members support each other in their development.

THERE NEEDS TO BE A FOCUS ON PERSONAL DEVELOPMENT, NOT JUST PROFESSIONAL DEVELOPMENT

Training in the human services should always include a component of personal development associated with professional development. The findings from this research suggest that the development of self-confidence in the participants enabled them to actually adopt specific case management skills learned in the classroom and apply these back in the workplace with improved service delivery to clients. It is unlikely that the same readiness to employ new skills would have been evident without the increased self-confidence. People working in human services require not only job specific skills, but also finely honed interpersonal communication skills for dealing with the wide variety of clients encountered in their daily practice. In order to provide a consistent quality service to each client, Case Managers need to be self-confident, know who they are, be self-aware and above all be centred in themselves – so they do not falter when a challenging situation presents itself.

ALL STAFF CAN DEVELOP AND RISE TO THE OCCASION, NOT JUST SOME

Much of the transfer literature advocates that only certain individuals are able to benefit from training and should be selected accordingly. The research findings from this study implied that this is not necessarily the case. The participants represented a wide variety of backgrounds, in terms of gender, ethnicity, age and level of education. In spite of this diversity, all participants indicated that they had experienced some personal and/or professional development, which in varying degrees has transferred back to the work environment. The use of an experiential/action learning approach enabled participants to experience learning opportunities, which were pertinent to their situation and develop from these learning experiences.

Implications for educational providers

EFFECTIVE EDUCATIONAL PROGRAMMES

This research suggests that experiential education can produce positive results for adult learners, particularly with respect to personal development. The use of an action learning approach provided a workable framework for focusing on not only personal, but also professional development. The integration of a university-based and work-based phase of the VUW Diploma in Rehabilitation Studies also appears to have been beneficial to participants. The time away from work enabled participants to reflect on their personal and professional lives, as well as develop networks with fellow ACC Case Managers from throughout New Zealand. The supervised work-based practicum facilitated the transition back into full-time work and provided opportunities for participants to put into practice what they had learned, by working towards personalised learning objectives, completing a case study and completing a research project. The final call-back module at Victoria University in Wellington consolidated the programme with participants presenting the findings of their research project and reviewing the learning from their learning objectives with their cohort colleagues as well as Principal Case Managers, Branch Managers, Regional Managers and representatives from Head Office.

Summary

The findings of this case study strongly endorse the notion that experiential course design, which bridges personal and professional development, will facilitate the transfer of learning from the classroom to the workplace. The value of preparation, the experience and reflective processes as advocated by Boud and Walker (see Figure 1.1) is also supported. The following chapter provides an insight into Cook Islands teachers' perspectives on the transfer of learning.

References

Accident Rehabilitation and Compensation Insurance Company (1995). Wellington, New Zealand.

Analoui, F. (1993). *Training and Transfer of Learning,* Avebury, Aldershot, UK.

Broad, M. L. and Newstrom, J. W. (1992). *Transfer of Training: Action-packed Strategies to Ensure High Payoff From Training Investments,* Addison-Wesley, Reading, MA.

Collinson, C. and Brook, J. (1997). Department of Psychology, Massey University, Palmerston North.

Denzin, N. K. and Lincoln, Y. S. (eds) (1994). *Handbook of Qualitative Research,* Sage Publications, Thousand Oaks, CA.

Gass, M. A. (1989). In *Adventure Education.* (eds, Miles, J. C. and Priest, S.) Venture Publishing Inc., State College, PA, pp. 199–208.

Gregoire, T. K., Propp, J. and Poertner, J. (1998). *Administration in Social Work,* **22,** 1–18.

Holton, E. F. I. (1996). *Human Resource Development Quarterly,* **7,** 5–21.

Leberman, S. I. (1999). *The Transfer of Learning From the Class-Room to the Workplace: A New Zealand Case Study.* Unpublished PhD, Victoria University of Wellington, Wellington, New Zealand.

Maier, H. W. (1994). University of Washington, Seattle, WA.

McGraw, P. (1993). *Asia Pacific Journal of Human Resources,* **3,** 52–61.

Seng, J. S. (1998). *Advances in Nursing Science,* **20,** 37–48.

Yin, R. K. (1994) *Case Study Research: Design and Methods,* Sage Publications, London.

5 Transfer of Training in a Cultural Context: A Cook Islands Teachers' Professional Development Case Study

The following chapter is an account of Lex McDonald's research that accompanied a teachers' in-service training programme, *The Cook Islands Teacher Development Project (Special Education)*, undertaken during the period 1995–2001. A full account of this research is available at www. vuw.ac.nz/education/staff/education-studies/lex-mcdonald.aspx

Context and overview

The Cook Islands Teacher Development Project (Special Education) over the period of the training was collaboratively developed by the Wellington College of Education, Polytechnics International New Zealand Limited, Psychlex Consultancy, the New Zealand Ministry of Foreign Affairs and Trade and the Cook Islands Ministry of Education. This teacher in-service programme was undertaken in response to an acknowledged need for teachers in the regular classes to be skilled in working with *all* learners (Cook Islands Ministerial Task Force, 1989; Densem, 1990; McDonald, 1995). The purpose of the allied research was to explore the cultural aspects of transfer of training in a specific setting and thereby uncover specific transfer of training strategies. Haskell (2001) noted that it was necessary to acknowledge the importance of cultural and context factors in transfer by stating 'it is clear, then, that cultures and contexts are powerful shapers of transfer' (p.149). Bridges (1993) commenting upon the transferability of skills in higher education has also recognised this need, arguing that 'we need to ask what would make one social context different from another to the extent that it might constitute a challenge to the transfer of skill' (p.49). This research was designed to contribute to the knowledge base of how culture impacted upon transfer and would therefore build upon the existing, but very limited, theoretical constructs in this area (for example, Lim, 1999; Lim and Wentling, 1998; Sarkar-Barney, 2001). In addition, Western models of training and practice were found to be fraught with difficulty in different cultural contexts (Bamford, 1986; Brady and Anderson, 1983; Jonsson, 1992; Thaman, 2001; Tupuola, 1993).

Hence, with the current worldwide interest in transfer of training, the increasing importance attached to the need for professional development programmes to impact and an acknowledgement of the complexities of teacher change, it was expected that this investigation on teacher in-service training in the Cook Islands would promote not only application implications – but also a much needed theoretical contribution on how culture can impact upon transfer of training. In specific terms then, the objectives of the study were:

1. The identification of appropriate and specific strategies for transfer of training that would

provide a basis for teachers, trainers and other significant people to work together to plan for effective in-service training.

2. An understanding of the overall patterns and themes associated with these strategies that would lay the foundation of an explanatory model. These patterns would also be useful for planning teacher in-service training and other professional development activities (with particular reference to the Cook Islands educational context).

3. The development and delivery of a teacher in-service programme that reflected the findings of these understandings; and,

4. To contribute to transfer theory with specific reference to how culture impacted upon transfer of training.

COOK ISLANDS CULTURE

In some sense it is difficult to define Cook Islands' culture as each island has its own culture and fiercely supports such differences. The Cook Islands has been a traditional society that embodies 'the Polynesian way' in which there are four key interactive elements that define such a society: kinship, status and respect, sharing and caring, and unity through consensus (Ritchie and Ritchie, 1985). It is grounded in the interweaving of the community, family and individual with an emphasis upon humility, Christianity, respect, hierarchical authority, consensus, peer group socialisation, the importance of the past and present, appreciation for privileges received, the values of friendliness and emotional spontaneity (Ritchie and Ritchie, 1979, 1985). The two key notions that govern behaviour are the concepts of *aroha* and *akama* (Cook Islands Maori). Aroha refers to love and a way of life, but it is more than this – it also implies a general concern for the welfare of others and is observed, for example, by kindness, greetings and farewells, trust, respect, loyalty and language. Akama is the other central concept. It refers to a personal state of shame and shyness of others as a consequence of a perceived wrongdoing by the person. It may result from peers and those in authority ridiculing the individual's mistakes or non-conformity. At times the implied criticism can be so strong that the person concerned may withdraw from interaction. The fear of it happening can become a powerful form of control.

THE COOK ISLANDS AND ITS EDUCATION CONTEXT

The Cook Islands is a tropical, self-governing nation and the people have a close affinity to the Maori of New Zealand. The current population is approximately 15,000 people, but extensive migration has occurred to New Zealand and beyond. It comprises 15 islands and is an independent country that has maintained close political links with New Zealand.

Educational resources and facilities are limited, however there is a teachers' training college and a few other tertiary training institutions. Rote learning has been a common teaching strategy (Jenkins and Singh cited in Davenport and Low, 2001), but increasingly aid-funded training has been utilised to promote teacher development. Indeed improved teacher performance has been one of the goals of the Cook Islands Education Ministry (Matheson, 1999), but improvement has not been ascertained, as valid impact data has not been collected. The education system has been very much influenced by New Zealand in terms of aid funding and educational personnel. The training programmes implemented with aid funding usually involve trainers from donor countries and an important consideration here is the skill of the trainers in cross-cultural contexts. For this project this was an important consideration although relatively little is known about inter-cultural training except that some general studies (for example, Benson, 1978) have identified *specific* behaviours and predictors of inter-cultural competency such as language skills, attitude, socially appropriate behaviours, friendliness and mobility.

THE COOK ISLANDS TEACHER DEVELOPMENT PROJECT (SPECIAL EDUCATION) AND TRANSFER RESEARCH

It was within this context that a teacher in-service education programme and accompanying research study was initiated in 1995 and concluded in 2002. The challenge was to adapt a New Zealand based inclusive education training programme (that emphasised the needs of students with special needs) for local teachers living in the Cook Islands so that there was a sustainable impact – the key objective being to develop procedures and strategies that were transferred long term to the classroom.

As the courses proceeded additional modifications were implemented and the concurrent research programme identified a range of issues and strategies that needed to be considered if transfer of training was to be effectively accomplished. This three-phased research project adopted a phenomenological case study approach and surveyed teachers, teacher educators and principals. Both qualitative and quantitative data were collected.

Findings

PHASE 1

Phase 1 was a prelude to phases in Phases 2 and 3 and was basically a direction-finder data collection phase. It was particularly important, however, because it highlighted not only important parallels with the international literature but also identified approaches that were considered important for teacher in-service transfer of training. Some allied preparatory studies identified appropriate contextual approaches for the study – Paterson (1994) developed a Cook Islands' in-service needs assessment tool and Sweeney (1994) identified a model for effective *papa'a* [European] interaction within that context.

During Phase 1, data was gathered to identify in-service training features that were favoured by the locals. There was an overall acknowledgement of the need for a relevant well-planned approach by the teacher and course developer. As one teacher commented about the course 'I might be doing things in the classroom, when there might be other ways to do things, to approach them, . . . I might learn something to help me'.

Professional development opportunities that promoted collaborative relationships and the opportunity to work together between the participants and others were favoured. Group activities and peer/staff co-operation were favoured with an emphasis upon action learning, development of practical knowledge, skills and resources, observational and case study learning and discussions. Back-up reading materials were also identified as being important, but lecture-type presentations were the least favoured. A supportive network, principal support and supportive attitude of the teachers' colleagues to the training were highly ranked. Self-selection for the workshop was also considered important.

With regard to trainer professional competency and administrative requirements, a number of characteristics were identified as being particularly valuable for course success. In particular, trainers who had a teaching background with a local and expert knowledge were preferred.

Morning courses, early in the year over a distributed time-period, along with a suitable venue (with resources, adequate food and drink) away from the school campus were important. Course handouts, resources to implement the course ideas and certification and/or monetary rewards were sought after as follow-ups to the training. Course evaluation was considered to be the responsibility of the trainers and the course participants and both summative and formative approaches were considered valuable. Most thought that feedback about evaluation should be made freely available. Additional data relating to teachers' preference for content and experience in special education was collected but is not reported on here.

In addition to the above data, comments were sought from a group of educators at a meeting to explain the project. Senior Ministry of Education staff and senior teaching staff identified a range of components important for in-service effectiveness: specific workshop methodology that emphasised practical and relevant action-based training with theory and practice links; the teacher as facilitator; the warm positive relationships between lecturer and teachers; a building of teacher's confidence; and teacher involvement in course planning and principal support. Some organisational and planning issues were also considered very important – there was a need to recognise the significance of the prayers, a suitable venue where food and drink could be readily accessed, and the specification of course requirements and a workshop that provided not only individual value but also community and national human resource development.

Classroom observations during Phase 1 by the research team produced additional data. It was observed that there were a lack of teaching resources and what existed was out-dated, in need of repair or inappropriate for the context. Student interaction was minimal and group work only occasionally occurred whilst the teacher was observed to be the manager of the knowledge.

The above data provided the foundation for the subsequent research. Although not markedly different in many respects to the existing literature and research on effective in-service training, there were some specific local needs and priorities identified along with cultural practices. The implication was of course that the trainer would need to be responsive to ideas that craft an effective in-service course and be particularly aware of ideas grounded in the cultural context. Because Phase 1 results piloted the research for Phase 2, the latter results will be considered before the implications for both phases are discussed in more detail.

PHASE 2

In the second phase of the research there was a more intensive search for the identification of the specific transfer factors. Teachers, teacher educators and principals identified a range of 116 before/during/after strategies and within each of these categories psychological, training, schooling and community factors were located. The facilitative and barrier items identified by the participants are detailed in Tables 5.1 and 5.2. Note that in Table 5.1 only the eight top ranked items are shown in the first two cells (trainer before and trainer during). For details on the other items please refer to the original study.

It was particularly evident that there were commonalities with the Phase 1 research data – there was an emphasis on items that were concerned with support/non-support (for example from colleagues, school, family, community), information sharing, collegial and principal involvement, recognition of effort, trainer professional and personal qualities, trainer contact, course methodology (particularly interactive strategies), relevance and benefit to school, sharing, teacher personal qualities, course notes and use of resources and facilities. Of particular note was the number of items relating to support (in terms of support *to* and *from* others), with

Table 5.1   Examples of some highly ranked facilitative strategies and the priority of cell categories*

	BEFORE	DURING	AFTER
TRAINER	Trainer provides content/method information Course requirements specified Course usefulness marketed Certificate provided for course completion Course material relevant Trainer has background knowledge Course will improve teaching Course benefits school/colleagues ** **Priority of Category: 10**	Course is well planned and organised Trainer contact during course breaks Training style satisfying Interactive training methods Teacher is rewarded for efforts Course material relevant to teacher In-course requirements specified Course helps teachers to network **Priority of Category: 7**	Trainer maintains contact Follow-up 'pep' course Training report to principal Reward/recognition provided ** **Priority of Category: 9**
TEACHER	Teacher flexibility Teacher shares ideas Teacher sets goals Teacher is confident Teacher is motivated Teacher chooses to attend Teacher relates easily ** **Priority of Category: 8**	Teacher flexibility Keeps course notes Evaluation by self/others Understands ideas Teacher is organised Participates in activities Relates to others easily ** **Priority of Category: 2**	Keeps course notes Evaluation by self/others Teacher's improvement personally rewarding Responsibility to implement new ideas Course book developed ** **Priority of Category: 3**
SCHOOL	Principal's involvement Colleagues' support School authorities support enrolment Staff consider course relevant ** **Priority of Category: 4=**	Teachers' colleagues are supportive Course ideas considered useful for whole school Principal supports/encourages School resources available to implement ideas ** **Priority of Category: 1**	Principal supports/encourages Course ideas etc. reflected in school planning Resources are made available for teacher use Benefits for school maintains teacher interest Continued collegial support to teacher Organised visits to other teachers ** **Priority of Category: 6**
OTHERS	Ministry support Family support Support (unspecified) for enrolment Community benefits ** **Priority of Category: 11**	Ministry support Family support ** **Priority of Category: 4=**	Ministry support Positive parent feedback Support from community ** **Priority of Category: 12**

Key: numerals (e.g. 11) refers to overall ranking; B = before; D = during; A = after; Tr = trainer; T = teacher;

S = school, work environment; O = others; Br = barriers; ** = no further ranking available

* For a detailing of all strategies refer to the original study

Table 5.2   Ranked barrier scores including priority of cell categories as determined by mean rank score

	BEFORE	DURING	AFTER
TRAINER	No course reward 57=(6BTrBr) Course at inconvenient time 79=(1BTrBr) Teacher does not get information 87=(10BTrBr) Ministry & principal don't get information 98=(8BTrBr) Trainer is too superior 100=(12BTrBr) Course requirement too demanding 100=(11BTrBr) Previous courses uninteresting 107(7BBrTr) Attending in hot weather 114(16(BBrTr) Trainer is not known 115 (15BBrTr) ** **Priority of Category: 8 (Mean Rank = 95)**	No trainer contact 61=(11DTrBr) Training programme is not helpful 73=(8DTrBr) Insufficient time to complete tasks 91=(1DTrBr) Course requirements too difficult 95=(10DTrBr) ** **Priority of Category: 4 (Mean Rank = 80)**	No follow-up contact from trainers 54=(4ATrBr) ** **Priority of Category: 1 (Mean Rank = 54)**
TEACHER	Teacher lacks confidence 102=(13BTBr) Teacher thinks they are too old 108=(14 BTBr) ** **Priority of Category: 12 (Mean Rank = 105)**	Too difficult for teacher to understand 57=(9DTBr) Teacher has personal difficulties 83=(9DTBr) ** **Priority of Category: 2= (Mean Rank = 70)**	Teacher insufficiently skilled 76=(12ATBr) Teacher has insufficient confidence 87=(10ATBr) ** **Priority of Category: 5= (Mean Rank = 81.5)**
SCHOOL	Other responsibilities at school 76=(2BSBr) Colleagues do not get information 104(9BSBr) Colleagues are critical 110(5BSBr) ** **Priority of Category: 9= (Mean Rank = 96.5)**	Resources are not available 67=(7DSBr) School does not support the teacher 67=(3DSBr) Teacher is over-worked 95=(13DSBr) Principal is not helpful 98=(4DSBr) Colleagues are not interested 108=(2DSBr) ** **Priority of Category: 6 (Mean Rank = 87)**	School does not help teacher 48=(2ASBr) Resources are not available 57=(3ASBr) Principal is not helpful 67=(11ASBr) No reward to continue 67=(5ASBr) Colleagues are not interested 79=(1ASBr) Demands placed on the teacher 83=(6ASBr) Students show little improvement 87=(9ASBr) ** **Priority of Category: 2 = (Mean Rank = 70)**
OTHERS	Teacher has family responsibilities 94(4BTBr) Teacher has another paid job 112=(3BTBr) ** **Priority of Category:11 (Mean Rank = 103)**	Other events interrupt participation 91=(5DOBr) Family do not support the teacher 105=(12DOBr) ** **Priority of Category: 10 (Mean Rank = 98)**	*Ministry policies do not support teacher 67=(7AOBr)* Events (e.g. cultural) cause implementation problems 116(8AOBr) ** **Priority of Category: 7 (Mean Rank = 91.5)**

Key: numerals (e.g. 11) refers to overall ranking; B = before; D = during; A = after; Tr = trainer; T = teacher; S = school, work environment; O = others; Br = barriers;
** = no further ranking available

the emphasis being upon a recognition of the importance of support and recognition from colleagues, principals, family and others.

Facilitative items were ranked higher than the barrier items and in general the 'during' and 'after' items were ranked as more important than the before items. This means that the participants considered the 'during' phase strategies particularly important, followed by the 'after' strategies and then the 'before' strategies. Table 5.2 highlights these findings. The identification of broad themes from this data followed. For a detailed account of these themes see Table 5.3, although in essence there were three meta-themes: teacher (course participant) qualities, facilitative trainer qualities and training strategies, as well as support to/from others.

Trainer, colleague and in-school support factors were identified as being important for effective transfer. Additional interviews were conducted to consider two central questions – what was the nature of social support for teacher professional development in the Cook Islands and what was the function of this support? Collegial and community (including parents, family and friends) support, although not always readily available, was considered to be particularly important as a motivational element and as a physical source of help. As one teacher observed 'I think the nice feeling is that they are letting you know that what you are doing is approved by other people'.

A key finding (also identified in Phase 1 research) concerned the function of the social support. It was noted that it had a key role in bringing about change in the classroom whilst its counter-point – criticism – was an impediment to transfer. The significance of support for personal growth and belief structures was noted, but it was indicated that support (given and received) had an added protective quality, in that it cushioned the impact of the adverse reactions of others. It acted as a mechanism to provide legitimacy to actions and thereby protected individuals from the criticism, gossip and contrary reactions of others. The senior/older teachers on a staff often were considered to be gate-keepers for innovation and frequently perceived to be reactionary and inflexible. Criticism from them made it difficult for the teacher to implement or continue to use new course ideas.

> I know islanders. Somebody goes up [that is teaching/outcomes improve]. We tend to pull them down. We tend to go and gossip ... and that puts you down. Sometimes you have this feeling why am I doing it?

> Just one single mistake you make and they jump on you and that is the fear of most teachers over here. Just to make a mistake and then everybody pull you down or criticise you. That's what it is, and that's why they need support ...

> Over here it's a big black mark [if you make a mistake] ... and over here you can't reason with some teachers. 'I'm right and that's it. Final!' There are no other options.

It was noted, however, that social support and fear of criticism was a complex issue and subject to a range of factors such as age, training, status of the individual in the school, family bonds and geographic location of the school.

There is considerable evidence gained from this research study that cultural issues need to be considered in planning, implementing and following-up courses. The findings in the first two phases of the study were consistent with one another in acknowledging culture as an important variable. It is, however, somewhat paradoxical that many of the features identified

Table 5.3   Themes, sub-themes and examples of participants' voices

THEMES	EXAMPLES OF RESPONDENTS' VOICES
Theme 1: **Teachers' individual qualities** – such as positive attitudes, ability to self-select for courses, able to set goals, demonstrate social skills, self-evaluation and feedback skills.	• Be genuine with yourself – that you are going in for something – and you set your goal that you are going to do it and do it right to the end and get good results from it. • Some teachers are probably just too scared to take the course ... it's probably an attitude problem – confidence – they don't have confidence in themselves. • We need teachers who are ... flexible to changes ... able to ... improve and willing to change their attitudes. • I think if we have good relationships between participants, then there is no animosity, no feelings of distrust, no feelings of fear – I think you create a better atmosphere. • The use by the school of retrained teachers as resource personnel, subject leaders, syndicate leaders, etc., during staff meetings ... [is to be recommended]. • The notes are important for planning. The principal wants to see them. • If a teacher can see it. It's worth my effort to do it and also if they get feedback from others who say; 'look it is an improvement' – from one of their students, from one of their colleagues. • It is difficult ... [in the school environment] ... where we train people and tell them to go back and train their staff and they find that very difficult, especially if you're the only trained one.
Theme 2: **Facilitative training structures/trainer** – such as management and administrative support, effective trainer, relevant course and supportive course	• [We need information] ... on what you are expected to do or to know and the relevancy of what you are going to do ... • I think that whoever comes here has got to have a pretty good idea of what it's like in our classrooms so they don't make assumptions about teaching that are not accurate. I think they have to have some ideas of what it is like to live here ... Like difficulties in actually living here ... by the time you get your planning done and cart your water from the creek and from the tank and community involvement. • ... the teachers have got to see the relevancy of the course ... they have got to clearly see the benefits that the course would either bring to themselves as individuals, as professionals and to the students they are teaching. • The teacher must participate actively, not just this lecture type of delivery ... [It is important to consider] ... the strategies, the techniques, being used and the understanding on the part of the deliverer that these guys do have difficulties and every now and then say 'look if I'm going too fast please stop me'.
Theme 3: **Support to/from** – such as school management, colleagues and community	• Actually we want them [i.e., colleagues] to support us. If they don't want to join into the course we would like their support if we are to do something in the school ... because there are times when we need them, when we need to ask their opinions ... there is often a lack of support within the environment, within the teaching environment. There's almost jealousy – not, not really jealousy; but there is a pull-you-down [attitude] which actually means putting it into place is not that easy. • Always my first thing is the family. [It] always keeps me going to this course, it's their support.

by the respondents are features recognised in the international literature as being priorities for effective in-service development, but there was no framework identified for sustained movement towards these goals. A deficit model of in-service training (OECD, 1998) was more apparent. The change processes were more marked by features of the normative cultural system. Emphasis was upon the importance of social interaction for learning with attention to collaborative, authentic and relevant activities. Personal, social and professional growth would occur as a consequence of this – in fact this is very consistent with the traditional means of learning in Polynesia – collaborative, participatory, observational and imitative learning are key features. Hence the importance of the respect relationship value between the course presenter and the participants – if there is a mismatch between the values and perceived authority of the trainer and trainees it can be problematic for learning. A trainer in this situation needs to bridge the gulf.

In the Cook Islands culture there is an emphasis upon collaboration, socially skilled behaviour, sharing, caring and interdependence of the individual with the community (Ritchie and Ritchie, 1985), and this is reflected in the data that has been gathered. Interaction with colleagues, the trainer, principal and the community were behaviours highly valued by the respondents. Relevance was another key issue, but it was a relevance that went beyond individual need. A course that was relevant to the whole *school*, its *planning*, the teacher's *colleagues* and the teacher's *own classroom* was important. The role x time dimensions of 'during', 'school' and 'teacher' (all very much socially mediated in the eyes of the participants) were particularly important aspects of the course process. This is somewhat at variance with the Broad and Newstrom's (1992) typology that stressed 'before' and 'trainer' elements.

Although the respondents identified a number of personal qualities that were considered useful to facilitate transfer, it was an important finding that many of these personal qualities and behaviours related to interaction with others and support to/from them (for example, sharing notes with others, being able to lead, to help others). The training strategies/methodology identified by the respondents provided a means of developing an understanding of how the respondents' ideas for transfer strategies were very much embedded in the culture. Group oriented training was preferred for helping all to learn and was viewed as a culturally normative motivating force (refer to the work of Wlodkowski and Ginsberg, 1995) to link individual with others whereas, there is some evidence (for example, Hynds, 1997; Tufue, 1998) to indicate that *papa'a* [European] learning in groups was more oriented toward individual gain. This process from a Polynesian perspective is a means of linking the individual and the group – Reissman (1965) argued that those who extend help often receive the greatest benefit and from the group perspective it ensured 'no animosity, no feelings of distrust, no feelings of fear' between course members.

In this study there was an emphasis upon explicit support from a wide range of sources: the school authorities, principal, colleagues, Ministry of Education, trainer and parents. It acted as a means of protecting the innovating teacher from criticism. In some senses it can be related to the strong peer group influence as a normative demand. *Akama* [causing shame] can occur in any setting if the normative behaviour is not evident – many teachers commented on their concern about the other teachers (particularly those who were perceived to have authority) in the school, who would be critical of innovation, experimentation and changes in teaching practice. *Aroha* is a balance for *akama* and is evident when group support is apparent. The teachers were seeking a supportive context for change something akin to the 'community of learners' approach detailed in the literature (for example, Darling-Hammond, 1998). Hence the importance of a collaborative, co-operative and group-centred approach to learning and the value of support given to others outside of the course – this assisted the teacher to comfortably move beyond the orthodoxy surrounding many teaching practices. The alternative is that many teachers may fail to implement and this then supports the deficit model of teacher in-service – the teacher fails to learn and implement and that teacher is then held accountable. Many of the barriers identified in the research study related to inadequate interaction or collaboration.

The first two phases of the research were concerned with the identification of specific strategies for transfer of training considered important for effective in-service training and the patterns of understanding about transfer that would provide the basis of a framework for an explanatory model. Some 116 facilitative and barrier items were identified and these were considered to be important explanations for the occurrence or lack of transfer of training. Overall what was most apparent was the central focus of the individual – community sense of self and the emphasis upon cultural values such as collectivism, caring for others and power distance. These findings corroborate the work of Sarkar-Barney (2001) that values were important for transfer.

PHASE 3

The third phase of the research evaluated the impact of a course which incorporated key social support (to and from others) teacher and trainer ideas identified during Phases 1 and 2. In particular the course emphasised strategies identified as important in the previous phases: provision of pre-course information, recognition for participation, group participation, support and feedback (for example, family, principal, collegial, Ministry of Education), facilitation of individual teacher involvement such as flexibility, a planned course programme that emphasised safe interactive training activities, trainer–participant interaction quality and trainer qualities and behaviours (for example, follow-up visits). Other effective training strategies were of course also implemented. Impact data was collected following this course.

Teachers were on the whole, highly satisfied with the course. Close to three quarters of the group scored the course at the highest level on a range of criteria. To what extent the teachers changed their conceptions of learning and teaching as a consequence of knowledge changes and experiences was another assessment undertaken. The results indicated that there was a movement away by almost all of the teachers from the notion that learning was an increase in knowledge, toward conceptions that emphasised deeper learning as the application of ideas and interpretive processing. Another assessment tracked teachers' conceptions about the nature of teaching and effective teaching. Many indicated that teaching had a dual function – it was a teacher centred/controlled activity and a facilitative-interactive process. Prior to the course many teachers focused on the teacher engaging the student in learning opportunities, whereas after the course emphasis was upon teacher operations and, in particular, the need for careful planning and the use of specific, effective teaching strategies. This was consistent with the objectives of the course – the teacher role needed to emphasise facilitation of learning rather than direct control of the learning. Teachers were also surveyed about their attitude to inclusive education. Over two thirds of them had a favourable attitude towards inclusive education practice prior to the course but by the end of it all (apart from two teachers who still favoured partial segregation) considered inclusive education a preferred option because they now had the strategies to deal with it.

> I think it is the most effective way of meeting ... [the needs] ... of children with special teaching needs. I think that by removing them from the classroom it will not help so they must be made

a part of each lesson, be given work that they are capable of doing. It is also the least expensive way of providing for their needs.

Knowledge development of the teachers was assessed by a number of means and it could be concluded that there were significant qualitative changes in the knowledge domain. Generally, prior to the course teachers emphasised *teacher* behaviours (for example, rewarding, locating activities at need level, having patience, speaking slowly, giving easier work), whilst the after the course responses identified these – as well as learning strategies and processes (for example, Bloom's (1987) thinking levels, co-operative learning and Gagne et. al's (1993) conditions of learning) and planning. A number of photographs taken during the course indicated changes in teacher behaviour and implementation of ideas in the classroom.

Assignments were analysed to measure the level of application of ideas in the classroom using a rubric adapted from the classification of the levels of transfer from Fogarty et al. (1991). Analyses of these 20 lesson plans indicated that by far the majority of the teachers were not only able to transfer the knowledge and procedures, but were also able to attain higher levels of transferability as measured by a transfer rubric. This rubric had four levels – overlooking (inappropriate use of ideas or little use), duplicating and replicating (copying of ideas and/or minor changes), integrating and associating (substantially new and different ideas introduced and/or new subject content with authentic activities) and innovating (divergent, insightful or novel use of the idea, skill).

Impact assessments were conducted at four months and then again at two years after this to ascertain the level of sustainability of the transfer of training. Data collected at the time of the first survey indicated very clearly that many ideas and strategies (for example, co-operative learning) were still being used, although planning type activities (for example, individual education plans) were mostly not being implemented. One of the principals noted:

There is a big difference in the classrooms for teachers who have done the course ... There are lots of displays in the classrooms and teachers are implementing co-operative learning. There is a lot of group work and teachers have adjusted their questioning mode ... Some of the teachers have changed the physical arrangements – they [the children] are now in pairs, groups ... The students enjoy the group activities ... it keeps them occupied, supporting, helping one another ... There is lots of sharing [by the teachers] and they feel much more confident, this is one of the reasons why they succeeded ... They talk about it at tea time ... 'I've done ... what have you done?' It's sharing. It's very good.

Implementation difficulties revolved around three issues – specific implementation task difficulties (for example, adaptation difficulty), lack of resources and insufficient time to implement. It was reported by the principal that there was no indication of ridicule, criticism or 'put-down' by any colleagues (course participants or non-participants) when new ideas were being introduced. In fact there was excitement.

The second assessment two years after the first indicated that teachers were still using many of the ideas and indeed many of the assessment and planning strategies were also now being used. The teachers reported that co-operative learning activities were very often still being used in the classroom. One of the principals observed:

To my knowledge the teachers are improving their teaching method, new resources are seen in the classrooms, working with groups, encouraging them to think for themselves. Peer tutoring is being encouraged and supervised. Happy faces are seen in the class which is comforting to know. Assessment is done orally – by checklist.

Some reservations were expressed however by another principal:

Some teachers are using 1–2 ideas which had worked for them. Planning and the implementing of their knowledge has been a weakness which I have found this year. So this last term has been concentrated on teacher unit planning to include all or some of the special education knowledge they have acquired.

Attitude changes had also persisted with many. One of the principals noted:

Some teachers have really changed in their attitude towards their classroom teaching practice. You hardly hear negative comments like 'upoko motini', [pumpkin head] etc. Some teachers' classrooms are colourful and full of students' work. Students seem less threatened and are freer to express themselves. This is almost certainly as a result of inclusive classroom course. They are using that knowledge.

A further measure was the degree to which teachers still found the material useful. The ideas of teaching strategies, lesson planning, terminology and defining special needs still had very high value, but the study of disability history and the value of parent involvement (this had not been widely practised in the past) was less favoured. It seems once again that the most readily transferred ideas were those that were practical and had significance for the teachers in terms of knowledge of the student, assistance with planning and suggestions for teaching strategies. Less practical information, or information that was contrary to teachers' experience, was not deemed to be as useful.

The key issue at this stage of the research was determining whether transfer was accomplished by the package of ideas that were developed for this specific course, in a specific context and at a specific time. There was ample evidence that this had occurred. But an important question to consider was to what extent these changes in behaviour, attitude, and so on would be maintained if the support was not maintained; the transfer techniques were only the vehicle to get to a destination – staying at the location involved more than this.

A transfer of training model

The purpose of this research was: to identify specific transfer strategies deemed to be useful in the Cook Islands context; locate any patterns and themes within these items and develop a model course drawing upon the identified strategies. In addition to this, and as a consequence of these developments, another purpose was to advance transfer theory with particular reference to an explanatory model that defines the importance of culture impacting upon transfer. Given that this research has clearly demonstrated the importance of culture impacting upon transfer, it is important however to consider other significant and relevant theoretical positions so that a meaningful, encompassing and comprehensive model can be developed.

A number of experts in transfer theory have recommended that a synthesis of theoretical positions can best explain how transfer is accomplished. A theoretical approach that can significantly contribute to this understanding is Haskell's (2001) multi-disciplinary, principles-based general theory of transfer. He has decried the extemporaneous approaches that have been developed and is scathing of the fads that have been applied to facilitate transfer. Haskell explains that what is needed is a theory that is based upon what we already know about learning and accordingly has outlined 11 widely accepted educational principles and related them to a general theory of teaching for transfer (see Chapter 2). The model that follows incorporates an adapted version of these principles. The Haskell model, which is grounded in theoretical principles, does not explain transfer in dynamic terms and accordingly the incorporation of models of the process is an important consideration. The approach developed by Baldwin and Ford (1988) emphasised the importance of the trainee characteristics, the training design and the work environment, contributing to the learning and subsequent generalisation. This model has had a significant impact upon the development of transfer research. Similarly, Broad and Newstrom (1992) developed a model that was based upon the establishment of a transfer partnership between the trainer, trainee and supervisor/manager but with each role contributing to the before, during and after training programme effectiveness. This approach highlighted the importance of defining transfer in terms of a process (as opposed to an outcome) and the work of Foxon (1994) further contributed to this understanding. In general terms, little attention has been directed toward how socio-cultural issues can impact upon transfer effectiveness. Accordingly, Analoui's (1993) socio-technical learning transfer model, which emphasised the importance of technical and social competence skills for transfer effectiveness was a somewhat considered contribution. Following this, Lim and Wentling's (1998) international model of training was considered unique because it was one of the first approaches to emphasise cultural factors interacting with the learning and work environments to impact upon transfer. From these models and the principles approach of Haskell a socio-cultural contextual model of the transfer process was developed (see Figure 5.1).

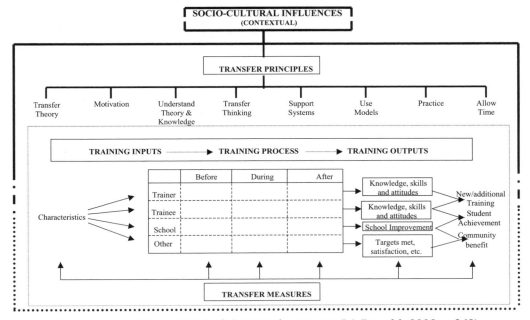

Figure 5.1 A socio-cultural model of the transfer process (McDonald, 2002, p.269)

IMPLICATIONS

There are a number of issues arising from this study that need to be considered in relation to the central finding that culture is an important variable in transfer.

1. The need to understand that cultural characteristics and values can significantly influence the outcome of training. It is also important to understand that an individual course participant is shaped by an interaction of political (for example, policy directives), economic (for example, available funding for resources), cultural (for example, attitude to authority), social (for example, degree of need for affiliation) and personal/psychological forces (for example, degree of motivational energy) and these intersect with the training programme and trainer. Thus the importance of trainers thoroughly understanding the local context and then demonstrating considerable skill in adapting the training programmes to meet these local needs. There needs to be a fit between the trainer and the participants and the local conditions. A trainer with content expertise is inadequate.

2. A central finding of this research relates to *support* for change. This notion is internationally acknowledged as a key determinant for effective change processes, but in societies in which there is an emphasis upon the co-operative and an avoidance of uncertainty this becomes even more crucial.

3. There needs to be an expectation of change when teachers are on courses. Teachers need to become change agents skilled in reflecting, adapting and innovating. Teachers need to have a means of dealing with resistances to change, when innovation is warranted, and an understanding that transfer of training depends upon a capacity to adapt content and methods with certainty.

4. Trainers working across cultures need to develop professional and personal cross-cultural expertise. Furthermore, the trainer needs to be fully aware of how best to integrate these skills with an appreciation of the political, economic, cultural and societal forces that shape the need for, design and implementation of the programme. Those in a training role working cross-culturally need a thorough preparation prior to entry and an ongoing development of skills if transfer is to be effectively managed. Research indicates that cross-cultural expertise is readily transferred to different settings given high levels of personal motivation.

5. Trainers need a clear understanding of how adults learn. 'In-service training' is better thought of as 'in-service learning' – there needs to be an emphasis upon training as a learning phenomenon. In particular, increased awareness of cognitive developments and the impact of culture upon learning needs to be strategically incorporated within the training programme.

6. There needs to be a careful interpretation of these findings as there are a number of potentially limiting factors. For example, it was an interpretivist approach and relies upon respondents and researcher interpretations of experiences and events. Phenomenological designs do not necessarily equate with truth, but of course obtaining an operational definition of truth is always a problem. Interviews are also problematic although triangulation of data was in many instances achieved. The relatively small number of respondents located within a specific environment implies that further research needs to be undertaken to consolidate the research findings, locate additional benchmarks and promote generalisability.

Summary

This chapter has outlined the role of culture in transfer as it relates to professional development in a Polynesian context. The findings from the study clearly endorse the value of Boud and Walker's (1990) model because preparation, experience and reflection were component parts of the professional development programme that ensured its success in impacting in the classroom. Furthermore, the development of the programme was somewhat consistent with the requirements detailed in the international literature on transfer, in addition to particularly important findings relating to the local context. The role of social support was highlighted as a key determinant of change in the setting and accordingly there was an emphasis placed upon 'know-with'. In the following chapter there is also an emphasis upon the understanding of learning and its relationship to transfer beyond the classroom and ensuring that impact of the learning is a preparation for future learning.

References

Analoui, F. (1993). Training and Transfer of Learning. Avebury, Aldershot, UK.

Baldwin, T. T. and Ford, J. K. (1988). Transfer of Training: A Review and Directions for Future Research. *Personnel Psychology*, **41**, 63-105.

Bamford, G. (1986). *Training the Majority: Guidelines for the Rural Pacific,* Institute of the Pacific Studies of the University of the South Pacific, Suva, Fiji.

Benson, P. G. (1978). *International Journal of Intercultural Relations*, **2**, 21–37.

Bloom, A. (1987). *The Closing of the American Mind,* Simon & Schuster, New York.

Boud, D. and Walker, D. (1990). Making the Most of Experience. *Studies in Continuing Education*, **12**, 61-80.

Brady, M. and Anderson, D. (1983). *Education*, **103**, 259–69.

Bridges, D. (1993). *Studies in Higher Education*, **18**, 43–51.

Broad, M. L. and Newstrom, J. W. (1992). *Transfer of Training: Action-packed Strategies to Ensure High Payoff from Training Investments*. Addison-Wesley, Reading, MA.

Cook Islands Ministerial Task Force (1989). Author, Cook Islands.

Darling-Hammond, L. (1998). *Educational Researcher, 27*, 5–10.

Davenport, E. and Low, W. (2001). *Basic Education and Pacific Peoples: Changing the Priorities,* Oxfam, Auckland, NZ.

Densem, P. (1990). Development Advisory Services for the Pacific. United Nations ESCAP, Vanuatu.

Fogarty, R., Perkins, D. and Barrell, J. (1991). *The Mindful School: How to Integrate the Curricula,* IRI Skylight, Palantine, IL.

Foxon, M. J. (1994). A Process Approach to Transfer of Training. Part 2: Using Action Planning to Facilitate the Transfer of Training. *Australian Journal of Educational Technology*, **10**, 1-18.

Gagne, E. D., Yekovich, C. W. and Yekovich, F. R. (1993). *The Cognitive Psychology of School Learning,* Harper Collins College, New York.

Haskell, R. E. (2001). *Transfer of Learning: Cognition, Instruction and Reasoning.* Academic Press, San Diego, CA.

Hynds, A. (1997). In *Wellington College of Education,* Wellington College of Education, Wellington, NZ.

Jonsson, T. (1992). Division of International Special Education Services, Newsletter, pp. 8–10.

Lim, D. (1999). Organizational and Cultural Factors Affecting International Transfer of Training. *Performance Improvement*, **38**, 30-36.

Lim, D. and Wentling, R. M. (1998). Transfer of Training Programs for Multinational Chain Hotels in Korea. *International Journal of Training and Development*, **2**, 17-28.

Matheson, K. (1999). Ministry of Education, Raraotonga, Cook Islands.

McDonald, B. L. (1995). Cook Islands Teacher Development Project: Project Plan for Teacher Inservice (special education).

McDonald, B. L. (2002). Transfer of Training in a Cultural Context. A Cook Islands Study. Unpublished PhD, Victoria University of Wellington, Wellington, New Zealand.

Organisation for Economic Co-operation and Development (OECD). (1998). *Staying Ahead. Inservice*

Training and Teacher Professional Development. Centre for Educational Research and Innovation, Paris, France.

Paterson, S. (1994). Wellington College of Education, Wellington, New Zealand.

Reissman, F. (1965). *Social Work,* **10,** 276–82.

Ritchie, J. and Ritchie, J. (1979). *Growing Up in Polynesia,* George Allen & Unwin, Sydney.

Ritchie, J. and Ritchie, J. (1985). Centre for Maori Studies and Research, University of Waikato, Hamilton, New Zealand.

Sarkar-Barney, S. (2001). Extending a Transfer of Training Framework to Include the Role of National Culture. Unpublished Doctoral, Bowling Green State University, Bowling Green, OH.

Sweeney, M. (1994). Wellington College of Education, Wellington, New Zealand.

Thaman, K. H. (2001). *International Education Journal,* **2,** 1–8.

Tufue, R. (1998). Wellington College of Education, Wellington, New Zealand.

Tupuola, A. (1993). *New Zealand Annual Review of Education,* **3,** 175–89.

Wlodkowski, R. J. and Ginsberg, M. B. (1995). *Diversity and Motivation: Culturally Responsive Teaching,* Jossey-Bass, San Francisco.

6 Transfer of Learning: A Case Study of Preparing for Future Learning

Transfer of learning is a fundamental assumption of educators. We trust that whatever is learned will be retained or remembered over some interval of time and used in appropriate situations.

(Ripple and Drinkwater, 1982, p.1947).

This chapter provides a summary of Stephanie's research into transfer of learning for business students. The study explored the experiences of a group of students who studied for a business degree by distance. The research was conducted in 2000–2001. In previous chapters we have established that transfer of learning occurs when a learner uses what has been learned in one setting in a new and different setting. The intention of all education and training is for learning to transfer, and yet there is much evidence to suggest that transfer of learning is difficult to achieve. It is crucial to develop an understanding of what helps and what hinders the transfer of learning from real learning situations to actual workplaces. The evidence from the case study discussed in this chapter was that general and specific transfer occurred for strongly motivated learners within a vocationally oriented distance education programme. A copy of a working paper based on her thesis can be downloaded from www.openpolytechnic. ac.nz/aboutus/research/otherresearch/distance+learning+doyle+s.pdf

Context and overview

The persistent problem for transfer of learning is whether or not general transfer occurs. Most researchers and practitioners would agree that specific skills and knowledge do transfer to similar situations. They agree that learners can achieve specific transfer, for example students learn Microsoft Outlook in class, and they then transfer what they have learned to other contexts at home or at work. The problem lies with transfer of generic skills to new contexts, and with generalising knowledge from one setting to a new and different context. For instance, the transfer of critical thinking skills developed on a course to a workplace context, or even the transfer of domain knowledge and understanding from a course to a significantly different context, such as the application of knowledge gained on a statistical analysis course to a business environment.

Whether we are talking about management skills or technical skills today or the workplace of the future, both need people who are deeply knowledgeable about their specific 'domain', and who have well-developed 'generic skills'. These generic skills include the ability to be flexible, adaptable, creative, think critically, problem-solve, have the skills required for learning and to transfer learning to new and different contexts.

Detterman (1993) distinguished between specific and non-specific or general transfer. When he talked of general transfer he was talking about the transfer of concepts, principles and strategies. In a stinging attack on general or non-specific transfer, Detterman argued that it rarely occurred and that therefore the focus should be on teaching the specific skills and knowledge to be used, not on teaching skills that learners would then have to work out how to use. Rather than supporting Detterman's argument, the case study discussed in this chapter provided ample evidence of general transfer of learning for a group of distance learners. The findings from the case study were consistent with the approaches to transfer discussed in earlier chapters, including the reconceptualisation of transfer as Preparation for Future Learning (PFL), and with the Good Shepherd theory of transfer.

The aims of the study were to develop an understanding of:

1.   The nature of transfer;
2.   Transfer of learning within the context of a distance education programme;
3.   Transfer of learning from the perspective of the students;
4.   Factors which facilitated transfer of learning from the Bachelor of Business to workplace settings;
5.   Barriers to transfer of learning from the Bachelor of Business to workplace settings; and
6.   Implications for designing and delivering distance education courses that nurture transfer of learning.

THE CONTEXT OF DISTANCE EDUCATION

As with the previous two case studies, this one also focused on the perspective of the learner, which has rarely been studied in terms of transfer. The context was that of The Open Polytechnic of New Zealand's (TOPNZ) Bachelor of Business, a distance learning programme. Distance education, with its potential to cater for high numbers of students, is one of the options policymakers and education providers consider when addressing the resource implications of the 'massification' of higher education and when catering for life-long learning. It is also an option considered by learners whose responsibilities preclude them from enrolling in a conventional lecture based programme. Given that transfer of learning provides the best measure of the effectiveness of any programme of learning, it is surprising that there have been few attempts to study it in a distance education context.

Since completing this research there have been a few studies which have considered the link between e-learning and transfer (Martin et al., 2003; Woodall, 2004). E-learning and distance learning have been heralded as the way to reach learners, traditional training options excluded. Despite this 'the growth and penetration e-learning has not fulfilled its predication' (Martin et al., 2003, p.229) in either Europe, or the United States of America. They attribute this to a range of factors including the way in which e-learning is delivered, the prior skills of the learner and the organisational support provided. For further discussion on e-learning as support for performance see Broad (2005).

The emergence of blended learning in recent years is an attempt to provide learning opportunities which maximise the potential of differing delivery styles, by combining online and face-to-face components in course design (Ausburn, 2005; Margaryan et al., 2004; Osguthorpe and Graham, 2003). Margaryan et al. (2004) reported that using e-learning on its own was not achieving the desired transfer of learning at the Open University of Shell Exploration and Production, and hence a blended approach using work-based experiences was introduced. They concluded that for transfer to be maximised the socio-cultural context was important, as well as a move away from a focus on content towards more process orientation. Similar conclusions were reached by Ausburn (2005), based on the feedback by university students participating in a course using blended learning. She concluded that 'adult students value course designs containing options, personalization, self-direction, variety, and an e-learning community' (Ausburn, 2005, p.327).

THE BACHELOR OF BUSINESS – THE ORIGINAL LEARNING CONTEXT

The Bachelor of Business (B.Bus) was established at the Open Polytechnic in 1992, and many of its first students had completed diploma level business qualifications with the Polytechnic. At the time of the study, the B.Bus had a number of majors including Accounting, Information Systems and Technology, Management and Communication. Accounting was the most popular major, and accounting majors were required to complete courses in accounting, law, management, communication and information systems and technology. Over 80 courses could be credited to the Bachelor of Business, however, the choices of students were more tightly circumscribed by the requirements of their major. A sample of five courses, two at 100 level, two at 200 level, and one at 300 level were selected for the case study. A number of the students had been enrolled in more than one of the sampled courses, and some had completed all five.

Usually students enrolled in this programme worked full-time and studied part-time. A full-time student could complete the 18 papers required in three years, but few were in that situation. The degree was offered over two standard semesters with a summer semester option available for a number of papers. Most students would take several years to complete the B.Bus.

The five courses sampled were all predominantly print-based and supported by a mixture of optional workshops, audio-conferences, email-based discussion groups, videos and CD-Roms. At the start of each semester students would receive pre-packaged course materials, with a course guide, tutorial assistance was available through a free phone and email service. A timely and comprehensive library service was also available for students.

The course experience of these distance students differed markedly from that of students in a conventional lecture-based programme. Distance students manage their own time, and have more freedom to decide what they study, when they study, and how they interact with the course material, their lecturers and fellow students. A student could complete the degree without ever having contact with teaching staff or other students. Or, the student may have chosen to have frequent contact with lecturers and to participate in all workshops, audio-conferences, list-servers and study groups.

The course requirements were similar for all the courses covered in the research. Four of the five had in-course assessments such as essays or projects and a final examination. The fifth course did not have an examination, but had four in-course assessments. The courses were designed to involve 180–200 hours of learning for the average student. Students were advised to spend 11–12 hours per week per semester for each course.

THE PARTICIPANTS

Thirty students or graduates from the B.Bus participated in in-depth interviews. They were a sub-group of the 245 who completed and returned an anonymous survey on experiences of learning and transfer. In comparison to full-time students at on-campus institutions most of those interviewed were older, with more than half the group being over the age of 35. Women slightly outnumbered men, and most of those interviewed were in full-time employment. The participants shared a strong vocational orientation, and often had multiple motivations for enrolling in the degree including:

- Seeking a credential (the degree and/or registration as an accountant);
- Able to staircase from the diploma;
- Second-chance education;
- Overcoming adversity (sickness, marital break-up, redundancy); and
- Changing career direction.

Most had been enrolled for at least two years prior to the interviews and a number had been enrolled for more than five years. At the time of the interviews 70 per cent were in full-time employment, with the employment situation being changeable for a number of the participants.

Findings

The interviews highlighted the diversity of experience and expectations learners bring to a single course, and the diversity of the contexts in which they are working and applying their learning. The following student did not have permanent employment, and usually had to apply her learning in non-business contexts. She describes using learning planning, goal-setting, problem-solving and research skills in her everyday life.

You tend – when you're on the benefit and when you've got children, and you've got all those sorts of conditions on you, you can get very focused on a very narrow path. And it helped me put my life in perspective, because I thought, 'well' – it made me look at five years down the track, ten years down the track ...

As an individual?

Yes, and plus, with the children – where would we be in that time? What planning had to go into action? Like, my son has decided that he will probably be doing sciences. He's fifth form this year. So I had to think, 'OK that's university, or if he can, through one of the Forces.' So we've put into place options that we've had to look at. And with my daughter, she's got a disability and she goes to secondary school next year. So we've had to look at secondary schools, how they've come out with the ERO [Education Review Office], how they handle that sort of problem. Do they handle that sort of problem? Class sizes, things like that.

These distance learners valued interactions with others in helping with learning and transfer, but not those with their fellow students. These learners integrated their learning with their everyday worlds, and not unsurprisingly they found interactions with friends, colleagues, managers and clients enhanced the likelihood of transfer of learning. One participant describes how she developed her interpersonal skills and tailored her communication so that she could get her needs for information met without alienating the people she was working with:

I certainly don't have enough knowledge to do it on my own, and not enough hands-on business knowledge. So I did have to talk to friends who were in business for themselves and who've never done any study and really think it's a load of old rot, but haven't been quite rude enough to say that. But you know, you get the idea from them. But because I was having to ask them questions and share what I was doing with them, I was taking a risk.

Many of the participants actively sought opportunities to apply what they had been learning to workplace problems and situations. For those working in accountancy positions there was plenty of scope to apply specific knowledge or skills to their work. But there were also opportunities to apply more general skills to workplace situations.

It's just like an idea – sometimes the opportunity for the idea to be applied – so then its, 'OK, what has to happen to make it a reality?' I try to do a lot of this myself if I can and I talk to other people about it. For example, at work at the moment we have an accounting software package but it is lacking a few bells and whistles. But at the same time our needs are quite unique. We can't necessarily just take another program because it wouldn't solve the problem. And so it's a matter of going through and researching and investigating. Talking – I think to my manager and the other person, the sales manager, I guess – about what we could do and trying to get a better idea.

The interviews with the learners in this case study provided ample evidence that most were effortlessly integrating their learning with their work. They reflected on what they were learning, most discussed what they were learning with their colleagues and managers and sought opportunities to apply their learning. Some courses, but not all, were designed to enable assignments to be based on real workplace problems and situations.

How the learners described transfer often conveyed a sense of new learning which was consistent both with what Perkins and colleagues (1991) called 'high road' transfer and with a PFL approach to transfer. For example, the following student's description of transferring what he had learnt on a course to a workplace situation moves from reflection and connection of new learning, to existing knowledge, through to learning more in order to apply the learning to the workplace situation.

Yes, you'd find your brain would wander off, and think, 'Oh yes, well, that's a bit what it's like at work.' And you'd put that into a context of – 'Oh, well, that could be why these things happen.' Or, 'Maybe the question we need to ask – of the organization is x, y and z.' So, more about questions, I think, rather than ...

When you say that – can you explain a bit more about questions?

Well, posing questions for yourself, I think, rather than – I mean, sometimes you might share them with your peers; at management meetings or something an issue comes up, we might – you know, 'I've just been studying this, and this came up'.

The learners thought that in order to improve learning and transfer the courses needed to be more closely aligned to workplaces. There were calls for greater use of practical examples and opportunities to use one's own work for assignments. Other suggestions made by the learners were for: more local content; small business examples; service sector and public sector examples; and keeping the course content up to date.

The findings of the study provide grounds for greater optimism about transfer than the literature would suggest. The study provided support for the broad outcomes claimed by higher education in general and TOPNZ for its B.Bus degree. The learners in the study reported that they had gained specific and general skills, knowledge and dispositions from their studies which transferred to their everyday lives. All could provide multiple and detailed examples of transfer of learning. Their degree studies made a significant difference to the learners' knowledge, skills and dispositions. For example:

> *I think just giving me more confidence in myself, understanding how people think, a lot of it, the communication skills. How the company runs its business – why we do things like we do.... I tend to sometimes be a bit more sheltered, and it's given me a broader understanding. I'm not afraid to go and ask.*

The learners reported that as a result of their studies they were more self-confident and open-minded, and held broader views of the world. In addition, they had learned to think more critically. The evidence was that those interviewed had grown in their skills as learners, and in awareness of how to be effective learners.

> *I'm more accepting, more willing to hear other people, not as hard-nosed as I used to be. More – I feel that I am able to listen and try and think through what other people are doing, looking at things more critically now than when I first started the degree. I sort of always had this sort of line in the sand, where everything was like YES-NO. Everything either fitted into the yes-no. It was either right or it was wrong. But when you are living in a situation which is constantly changing, you have got to recharge, change your thinking and the way you do things. Things are not as clear-cut as that. I do think, I do think things through more critically, more patiently probably than I used to.*

What was surprising in the light of the literature was the range and depth of examples of transfer provided. The examples highlighted the value of linking learning to real workplace problems and situations. Workplace problems are usually complex and a problem-solver needs to integrate and adapt learning from a range of sources to address them. One of the participants described bringing together learning from information systems, accounting, business management and communication courses to put a debt management system in place for the organisation she worked for:

> *What I actually had to do was to put in place a system whereby we reduced our debt level and we managed our debt – our bad debtors. So I had to put in place a system – so that was the information systems paper. I had to put in place an accountability process, a paper trail whereby the process of warnings was recorded and that people's accounts were adjusted accordingly, and the business management in terms of letters that we sent out to people. And how we managed the meetings we had amongst the four of us when we discussed what to do about the people who were not responding.*

When participants applied what they were learning to real problems and situations they appeared to engage in deep learning, rather than surface learning. As a result, they grew in confidence and clarity about what they were learning, and what the future applications of that learning might be. The evidence suggested that their formal learning assisted participants in recognising the learning that lay hidden in earlier workplace experiences. This could be categorised as the 'Aha!' factor: 'Aha! That's why that happened.'

> *Yes, it is, it's just interrelating the people, concepts, ideas, seeing it first-hand, then when you do the degree course and go over it, a lot of the times you're going through it, the old light switches*

on, you go, 'Oh yeah, I can relate to that. Yeah, I remember an incident that happened.' It just puts things more in the picture.

It appeared that, not only was current learning organised and stored for future retrieval, but that inert knowledge was re-organised and re-stored and thus made accessible for future learning. The evidence suggested that the opportunities to reflect on and apply learning at work may have nurtured dispositions and habits which were conducive to transfer.

The evidence from the case study suggests that the instructional approaches used on the B.Bus were supportive of transfer. But, it should be noted that few examples were provided of complex transfer. Instructional approaches were discussed with the staff who had been involved in course development and with teaching on the courses. Once specific and general learning outcomes were identified for a course, the focus of the instructional design and teaching team members appeared to be on how to cover the curriculum and how to best prepare students for assessments and examination(s). Scant attention was paid in designing instructional activities to future applications of the learning. There was no evidence of research or feedback from learners as to their experiences with application some time after completing the course. It is, therefore, likely that design and teaching team members relied on their own experiences and anecdotal information from students.

The only feedback referred to by staff was the end-of-course student evaluations, and the formal course evaluations. Almost no reference was made to transfer in these evaluations, or in the staff members' comments on the evaluations.

THE NATURE OF TRANSFER

The first objective of this research was to develop an understanding of the nature of transfer. In the study reported here, transfer of learning was conceptualised within a constructivist view of learning anchored in cognitive psychology (Bransford and Schwartz, 1999; Gagne et al., 1993; Singley and Anderson, 1989). A cognitive constructivist approach is one in which learning is an individual process. Transfer of learning is an iterative process. All learning requires some degree of transfer.

1. Each learner brings to the learning situation their pre-existing knowledge schemas, orientations or motivations and their preconceptions as to the future transfer of that learning (see Chapter 2).
2. In order for new learning to occur the learner needs to process the new 'data' through their pre-existing knowledge schemas and in so doing both the new and the existing knowledge are transformed (see Chapter 2).

We referred previously to the emerging consensus among transfer of learning theorists as to the pivotal role which encoding and organisation of knowledge plays in the accessibility and retrieval of knowledge in new and different situations. If knowledge is encoded and stored for the end-of-course examination questions, or to address an essay topic, then they are the future uses for which knowledge will be available. Importantly, if knowledge is encoded for future use in addressing workplace problems which are typically ill-structured and multidimensional, then that is how the knowledge will be encoded and organised, and the type of situations that it will be accessible for. In essence, this is a cognitive explanation of meaningful learning enabling generalisation to unpredictable future situations.

This conceptualisation of transfer places considerable emphasis on the prior learning and motivations that learners bring to the learning experience, and the way these contribute to the construction of learning. To paraphrase Perkins and Salomon (1989), such learning is in part 'backward reaching'; it is also 'forward reaching' in relation to the transfer situation – reaching forward to the future.

The study identified few examples of more complex transfer. Complex transfer requires what Perkins and colleagues refer to as far-reaching high road transfer, which relies heavily on metacognitive skills and requires creative, adaptive and innovative thought from the learner. Larkin (1989) referred to transfer as requiring 'new learning'. Bransford and Schwartz (1999) reconceptualised transfer as 'preparation for future learning' (PFL). Detterman (1993) and many others deny the probability of general transfer; and yet, it is the form of transfer increasingly being sought from tertiary education providers.

An important component in preparing for future learning is knowing how to set up the 'transfer' situation for learning. This entails identifying resources, setting up networks, and being able to ask effective questions of others in order to access support and thus facilitate new learning. Activities which make the value of such actions explicit and provide opportunities for learners to set up situations, which support their learning, need to be incorporated into the instructional design.

Implications for course design and delivery

There is a growing literature providing sound guidelines for factors which enhance teaching and learning for transfer (Bransford and Schwartz, 1999; Ford and Weissbein, 1997; Haskell, 2001; Misko, 1995; Perkins, 1995). The insights gleaned from the current study on factors facilitating transfer of learning were consistent with the literature.

If the potential of learning to transfer is to be realised, then transfer needs to be specifically attended to. This is not a novel view, but one which has a history within the study of transfer including Ellis's (1965) suggestions for teaching for transfer; Fogarty and colleagues (1992) call for a 'shepherding of transfer'; Sternberg and Frensch's (1993) suggestions for teaching for transfer; and Haskell's (2001) 11 principles for transfer. In addition to attending to transfer within the design of courses, there is a need for learners to have specific instruction on effective strategies for learning and transfer. The current study identified a number of factors which are important to teaching and learning for transfer and which were not adequately addressed within the courses. These included:

- The prior learning and experiences of learners;
- The expectations of learners;
- Current work and life situations;
- Multiple examples (with diverse contexts); and
- Future (and diverse) applications of the learning.

There is strong support for using authentic and personally meaningful situations to foster deep learning and transfer of learning. The findings of this research emphasised the need to create opportunities for learners to actively engage in shaping their own learning. Deep learning occurred when the course enabled the students to integrate their learning and their living through the use of real work problems and situations. It is acknowledged that such an approach requires more effort from all parties, than does the current situation.

An increased focus on transfer needs to be built on evidence from practice, and specifically from evaluations of the after-course experiences of students. The current gap is in knowledge and understanding of both the contexts that learning will be applied in, and of the experiences of the students when they come to apply their learning some time following the course. Design and delivery of the courses such as the B.Bus would be enhanced if they were informed by evidence from such evaluations.

In common with traditional approaches to education, Bransford and Schwartz's PFL approach shares an emphasis on the necessity for solid content knowledge and understanding of underlying principles. Where it differs is in its 'knowing with' perspective, which requires learners to notice and interpret. In the learning context, learners are encouraged to generate their own thoughts on problems and then to compare those to the thoughts of experts and others. The PFL approach emphasises the importance of learners learning how to ask appropriate questions, being able to reason, and engaging in reflective thinking. Learners need to be provided with exemplars of effective questions, of engaging in reasoning (for example, the think aloud protocols of cognitive apprenticeships), and of reflective thinking. The challenge for distance educators is to provide feedback and guidance to students in their own attempts at asking questions, reasoning and thinking reflectively.

The apparent failure of transfer of learning from educational contexts to different settings, is in part a consequence of the lack of connection between the initial learning situation and potential transfer situations. The use of experiential learning approaches enables the integration of learning and living. The student is facilitated in integrating what is learned into their everyday practice. Habits, such as self-management and critical reflection, are cultivated within authentic out-of-course contexts. Such experiences are in keeping with Bransford and Schwartz's (1999) PFL approach to transfer, in that the learning experiences are critical, and based on authentic problems which typically require new learning. In such approaches transfer of learning also involves additional learning from others (such as colleagues), and these experiences nurture the internalisation of learning, thus making it more accessible for future situations.

The view of transfer that emerged from the study could be termed 'learning for transfer'. In this view, the initial learning experience(s) shapes the potential for transfer. This occurs on a number of levels. The existing knowledge schema the learner brings to the situation filters the new knowledge while being transformed by it. If learning within a course is shaped around authentic applications and future transfer then that is how the knowledge will be encoded and how it will be available in the future. On another level there is the preparation for future transfer which is about developing metacognitive awareness and the skills of learning to learn (which are mirrored by the skills of learning to transfer). Associated with these are the dispositions, or the dispositional knowledge, which are required for transfer – 'the spirit of transfer'.

Summary

The findings from the case study of the experiences of distance learners enrolled in a Business degree supported the re-conceptualisation of transfer as preparation for future learning. The case study demonstrated that distance education facilitates transfer through enabling the integration of learning and living. The findings recognised the importance of addressing transfer of learning as a core outcome to be explicitly addressed in the development, delivery and evaluation of all educational courses and programmes. Transfer is crucial to understanding learning, and vice versa. Chapter 7 highlights three factors which have been identified in the literature and confirmed in the case studies, as facilitating transfer – learner characteristics, course design and the work environment.

References

Ausburn, L. J. (2005). *Educational Media International, 41,* 327–37.

Bransford, J. D. and Schwartz, D. L. (1999). *Review of Research in Education, 24,* 61–100.

Broad, M. L. (2005). *Beyond Transfer of Training: Engaging Systems to Improve Performance,* Pfeiffer, San Francisco, CA.

Detterman, D. K. (1993). In *Transfer on Trial: Intelligence, Cognition, and Instruction.* (eds, Detterman, D. K. and Sternberg, R. J.) Ablex Publishing Corporation, Norwood, NJ, pp. 1–24.

Ellis, H. C. (1965). *The Transfer of Learning,* The Macmillan Company, New York.

Fogarty, R., Perkins, D. and Barell, J. (1992). *The Mindful School: How to Teach for Transfer.* Hawker Brownlow Education, Highett, Australia.

Ford, J. K. and Weissbein, D. A. (1997). *Performance Improvement Quarterly, 10,* 22-41.

Gagne, E. D., Yekovich, C. W. and Yekovich, F. R. (1993). *The Cognitive Psychology of School Learning,* Harper Collins College, New York.

Haskell, R. E. (2001). *Transfer of Learning: Cognition, Instruction and Reasoning,* Academic Press, San Diego, CA.

Larkin, J. (1989). In *Knowing, Learning and Instruction: Essays in Honour of Robert Glaser.* (ed., Resnick, L. B.) Lawrence Erlbaum Associates, pp. 283–305.

Margaryan, A., Collis, B. and Cooke, A. (2004). *Human Resource Development International, 7,* 265–74.

Martin, G., Massy, J. and Clarke, T. (2003). *International Journal of Training and Development, 7,* 228–44.

Misko, J. (1995). *Transfer: Using Learning in New Contexts,* National Council for Vocational Educational Research, Adelaide, Australia.

Osguthorpe, R. T. and Graham, C. R. (2003). *The Quarterly Review of Distance Education, 4,* 227–33.

Perkins, D. N. (1995). *Outsmarting IQ: The Emerging Science of Learnable Intelligence,* The Free Press, New York.

Perkins, D. N. and Salomon, G. (1989). Are Cognitive Skills Context Bound? *Educational Researcher, 18,* 16-25

Ripple, R. E. and Drinkwater, D. J. (1982). In *Encyclopedia of Educational Research,* Free Press, New York, pp. 19–48.

Singley, M. K. and Anderson, J. R. (1989). *The Transfer of Cognitive Skill,* Harvard University Press, Cambridge, MA.

Sternberg, R. J. and Frensch, P. A. (1993). In *Transfer on Trial: Intelligence, Cognition and Instruction.* (eds, Detterman, D. K. and Sternberg, R. J.) Ablex Publishing Corportion, Norwood, NJ, pp. 25–38.

Woodall, J. (2004). *Human Resource Development International, 7,* 291–94.

7 *Facilitating Transfer*

This chapter provides an overview of the main factors facilitating the transfer of learning, focusing on the learner, the course design and the workplace. Each factor is introduced and then highlighted with examples from the case studies discussed in the previous three chapters. Boud and Walker's (1990) model for promoting learning from experience encapsulates these three areas in both the preparation and experience stage of the model, with the reflective processes providing the mechanism for the learning and transfer to occur.

Pertinent to the three areas of learner characteristics, course design and work environment is the concept of individual culture. The importance of the learner's culture has received little attention to date as discussed in Lex's case study, but there is a growing realisation that an acknowledgement of cultural factors can have a significant facilitative effect on transfer. It has been argued throughout this book, and emphasised in the case studies, that transfer of learning does not just happen, it needs to be purposively planned for by teachers and learners.

Learner characteristics

There is an increasing awareness of the importance of cognitive processes to transfer. How the learner encodes and organises knowledge is very significant for its later accessibility, retrieval and use. This means that if educators and trainers want learners to be able to transfer learning to new and different contexts, then they need to address cognitive processes in their instruction design. This requires considering the encoding, organisation and retrieval of knowledge.

The review of the transfer of training literature discussed in Chapter 2 divided trainee characteristics into three different areas, ability and aptitude, personality – including a high need for achievement and an internal locus of control, and lastly motivation. Examples in the motivation category included confidence, high self-expectancies, high job involvement and a strong belief in the value of training. Some of these points were highlighted by the participants from the research with teachers in the Cook Islands (see Chapter 5):

> *I think one important factor is attitude. They need to know what it is they are doing and also be interested in the welfare of the students.*

> *We need to be able to improve and change our attitudes.*

> *I think the teachers have got to make sure they understand ... how the process goes. I think they have got to understand thoroughly.*

When transfer is regarded as an ability, rather than a process, it is learned intelligent behaviour, which prohibits transfer from one situation to another taking place, as discussed in Chapter 1. In essence, they have not learned to think, but have learned to reproduce their knowledge, which necessarily limits its application to different contexts. Similarly, the ability of the trainee to determine correctly the level of support they will receive on return to the workplace, may affect their efforts to apply their newly learned behaviours. This point was emphasised by a participant:

If the principal is made aware I can become a resource person for the teachers, then benefits can be given to others in the school.

The students who successfully transferred learning from the business course discussed in Chapter 6 were prepared to innovate, to be creative, and to draw on diverse sources of knowledge. Typically, complex transfer did not occur automatically, but required effort. The student would make a connection between prior learning and the current workplace problem. He/she would then draw on a wider set of resources: books, course notes, colleagues and knowledge of the workplace environment to adapt learning to the workplace problem.

In Chapter 5, the teachers were also very aware of the need to consolidate and extend their learning. This was frequently undertaken by sharing ideas and practising with other teachers. As one participant stated:

We frequently talk about the ideas and share them with others who haven't been on the workshop. In this school we have worked with one another to try the ideas out and at the end of the lessons we talk more.

The learner is also applying what they have learnt in the way of critical thinking, problem-solving and how to ask questions that will assist with the new learning required in the transfer situation. They are learning 'with' their prior learning and experience. This is consistent with Bransford and Schwartz's (1999) view of transfer as 'preparation for future learning' and Boud and Walker's model of promoting learning from experience (see Figure 1.1).

The importance of learning about the backgrounds of adult students prior to commencing teaching was highlighted by the teachers from the Cook Islands, and is exemplified by the following observation:

You need to make sure you come here and observe the teachers before the workshop. You need to observe them in a classroom. It is a different environment to your environment. You will need to know how they react to certain suggestions and things like that before you actually start thinking about what will be the content of the course. You need to understand the local flavour, the local context, the teachers' aspirations, their problems and difficulties.

In the Cook Islands study there was also considerable agreement that motivation of the course participants before, during and after the workshop was an important determinant of transfer. As one participant in the study noted:

I think the teachers have got to be motivated. An important factor is the attitude of the teacher, they need to understand themselves what they are doing and be interested in the success of their students.

Another participant, in commenting upon the teacher's confidence and capability to achieve, stated that setting personal goals and commitment was an important consideration.

The course participant needs to be genuine and honest with themselves ... there needs to be a realisation that there needs to be an achievement ... goals needs to be set so that good results can be achieved.

One of the business students, from the case study in Chapter 6, was confident he used much of what he learned in courses at work. While he did work in an accounting role, his description of using skills and knowledge from accounting courses demonstrated a significantly higher level of cognitive processing. He clearly integrated learning, and consciously set about interpreting new information or learning in the light of existing knowledge:

I've used the accounting. I'm now in a situation where, in an hour's session, I have the ability to get as much information from a client as possible. So I'm getting all the financial information from them and it's the ability to come back and interpret that. And I mean, in accounting, you're hopefully working with the company, financial results, in an automatic way, or have the ability to get some information and the rest of it I just try and decipher from the client. And then bring that back and put that together so I understand their position. And then, 'How are we going to contribute to that?' and, 'What are we going to cost our client?' And making sure we've got our numbers right, that we're going to make the revenue from that. It's probably not using to the nth degree some of the accounting packages, but it's using the templates, the way they'll logically go through the different parts of the business and establish costs.

Related to self-confidence is self-esteem. Self-esteem is arguably about connectedness, a sense of uniqueness, a sense of personal power and a sense of purpose. One of the Case Managers from the research reported in Chapter 4 emphasised this point by commenting that:

I took my increased confidence back to the office and after a couple of weeks I realised that I needed to make some changes regarding my workload. There was no support from team leaders so I went on my own initiative due to my increased self-confidence. I led by example. The mere fact that what I was doing was working meant that others followed suit, particularly with respect to working with employers. My positive attitude flowed on to other people.

The learner focuses on determining what is important and identifies meaningful connections, to him or herself, from ideas, stimuli and learning. Another participant observed that:

My confidence has increased and also before the course I was very much a black and white person, now I'm much more creative. I'm more focused on needs assessment rather than the client fitting the legislation. I find a part of the legislation that fits them. Confidence and self-awareness were key factors in enabling me to apply for new positions. Knowing that if you set your mind to it you can do it – nothing is impossible. Just like the first assignment, I never thought I'd finish it.

In the Cook Islands study teacher risk-taking was also considered a priority. It was identified by many of the participants that the teacher who is transferring ideas from the course to the classroom needs to be willing to try new ideas, be flexible and able to change and modify attitudes and approaches. But there was an acknowledgement that this might be at a cost. As two participants commented:

With regard to putting ideas in place, I think teachers should ask more questions about what is meant to happen, they need to keenly observe, attend to learning the task, think about trying all the ideas and then try some in the classroom.

There is often a lack of support within the teaching environment ... there is almost jealousy ... there is a pull-you-down attitude which actually means putting into place is not easy.

Risk-taking in the managerial setting is also pertinent to this discussion. Within case management Case Managers are called upon to make decisions, often involving large sums of money, where the outcome is often uncertain, as highlighted in Chapter 4. This means that managers need to know about and understand the process of decision making involving risk, rather than try and avoid situations where risk is involved or alternatively being too overconfident where risk is an issue – in essence have a clear understanding of risk management principles.

Course design

If a course is designed to prepare learners for examinations, then knowledge will be encoded and stored for retrieval in composing essays, or for answering exam questions. The learner may effectively transfer the learning within the examination or essay situation, but is likely to have difficulty with transfer of the learning to a workplace situation. If a course is to prepare learners for future workplace situations, then the learner needs to be prepared to draw on a range of resources and to adapt learning to complex and ill-structured workplace problems. The educator or trainer will need to facilitate the encoding of knowledge for use in authentic problem-solving, or for use in identified situations in the future. Later, the learner will 'know' with knowledge that is encoded, organized and can be retrieved for workplace problems.

When learners in the business degree were asked what helped them transfer learning, many emphasised the relevance and usage to their work. One accounting student described it this way:

The ones where I retain the information it does stick with you. I keep going back to the tax and auditing but it is something that I use all the time.

The Cook Islands educators also considered relevance an important issue. It went beyond personal relevance however, as evidenced by the following comment:

... the teachers have got to see the relevancy of the course ... they have got to clearly see the benefits that the course would either bring to themselves as individuals, as professionals and to the students they are teaching ... and ongoing benefits will come back into the classroom and into the school itself. Our colleagues will benefit.

The experiences of the business students suggest that repeated practice in real situations provided opportunities to gradually build on and extend the original learning in a relatively effortless way. It is common for school children to extend their skills reading and writing in a similar way. They may 'formally learn' to read and write in specific classes, but gain fluency through applying that learning in multiple and diverse contexts. Sometimes the learning that is transferred is learning how to go about learning in a new situation. One of the participants in the case study detailed in Chapter 6 said the following.

A lot. There's no way I could do that if I hadn't done the degree. I would be stumbling through not doing very well at all ... If I want to know something, or if I want to learn something I know how to go about doing it. Simple things like – if I am going to the library for example – I know how to get the information I want rather than fumbling around maybe getting this and maybe getting that – it's more – I guess when I do something it is in a more direct, focused way.

Another of the participants from the same study described this process as follows:

Well, the guy I work for, because he's sort of a developer, and he buys a lot of buildings to rent out, like he's just bought this big building in the city that covers a block. And it's leased out to a big timber company. But with him – I'm trying to think of a specific. There are things with him where I've said to him, 'I'll go home and get my books out, because there's laws on that.' And just with even partnerships and company law ... Even like – there were some environmental issues and things with the timber processing. And it's been really, really helpful.

One of the Cook Islands teachers related the motivation to continue using the ideas to being aware that there was an improved performance by stating:

If a teacher can see the improvement ... It's worth the effort to do it ... also if they get feedback from others or from their students ... they will continue to use it.

The Cook Islands participants favoured an off-site workshop, but with access to resources from their school (for example implementing the ideas in their own classroom) to support their learning. They could see the benefit of using both locations to advance their learning and use of ideas. This is highlighted by one of the participants:

It's best if we work at the Teachers' College ... away from our school ... we can get involved in the problems at school if we don't have the course away from the school ... but its good to go back and try the ideas in my class and with my buddy.

As argued in Chapter 3, using an experiential learning approach in particular, action learning, enables the use of an appropriate teaching methodology. This transfer of theory to practice was highlighted by one of the Case Managers as follows:

Being able to put theory into practice. The way we learnt what we did. When I think about the best way I learn it is by discussion, by doing, working through ideas and then applying them to the situation, because it is easier to then transfer it back to what I was doing here. Also the discussions we had in the classroom and regional groups.

Similarly, it is suggested that appropriate, but diverse, activities are designed. This point was emphasised by a Case Manager by stating:

Now when I'm faced with ugly situations I reflect back to the critical incidents. How not to lose my cool and knowing that the result of the interview would set the scene for outcomes in the next six months. I also imagined the others were watching me.

A mixture of assessment, to match the variety of learning styles represented in the students is also advocated. For example, the use of journal writing is supported in the experiential learning literature as a form of assessment, conducive to developing skills in reflection. Two participants from the study in Chapter 4 provide support for using an experiential approach:

I've had on-site meetings with claimants about six at a time and established rapport. It got quite aggro once I was inside, but now they are aggro at the system not at me, as they are no longer dealing with a faceless organisation. I link it to going onto the marae and not knowing what would happen. I'm meeting with them on their terms, going to their factory, wearing a collar and tie (I put a jersey over the top) and meet in their smoko rooms. It was nerve racking but very worthwhile.

The cultural side made me much more aware of not just different coloured skins. I now visit new claimants in the first seven days. I learn about their homes, find out about how they live, as you get used to white middle class living, but people live very differently. I now also dress more casually and am accepted more easily.

The business degree, described in Chapter 6, aimed to develop the problem-solving skills of the students. One of them recounted how he transferred or applied his developing problem-solving skills.

It's just like an idea – sometimes the opportunity for the idea to be applied – so then its, 'OK, what has to happen to make it a reality?' I try to do a lot of this myself if I can and I talk to other people about it. For example, at work at the moment we have an accounting software package but it is lacking a few bells and whistles. But at the same time our needs are quite unique. We can't necessarily just take another program because it wouldn't solve the problem. And so it's a matter of going through and researching and investigating. Talking – I think to my manager and the other person, the sales manager, I guess – about what we could do and trying to get a better idea.

This was also mentioned by a Case Manager:

Giving presentations was important to me as you learned how to structure them and use the appropriate resources. I give a lot of presentations in the community and to the public – so it was very helpful.

The value of taking non-physical risks has been discussed in Chapter 3. It is acknowledged that the propensity for taking risks needs to be seen in the context of encouraging course participants to take calculated risks, which have been considered within a risk management framework. A teacher from the Cook Islands observed:

We teachers need to try ideas ... work with others and put them in the classroom ... you [the trainer] can only go so far and the rest is up to us.

Developing a peer support network of fellow students was regarded as important by the participants. This was in evidence for the Case Managers, as one participant observed:

There have been radical changes in the branch over the past twelve months with ideas coming from myself and others. The single most influential change has been instituting case conferencing. We've also reduced case loads from 257 to 128 per case manager, due to a change in the way we work. Each case manager focuses on five people per month, like we did for the case study during the practicum. This has led to making a real change in the community. Case managers make their choice based on professionalism. Working with post 52 week people or people at 13 weeks who might need more intensive work is encouraged. The staff were not overly keen on all the new ideas mainly due to their worrying about time. Now the people are happy with both case conferencing and supervision. They see the case conference as a learning opportunity. There is also more helping and sharing in the case management team. People will now ask for help due to the safe environment which has been created.

The Cook Islands participants were very keen to share and buddy ideas. A number were keen to visit others who had previously undertaken the course and learn from them.

We need to have visits to other teachers who have completed – this will keep our interest up and we can see the ideas in the classroom being used.

The concept of a relapse prevention module to prepare course participants for their return to the workplace, was endorsed by participants. It seeks to identify some of the difficulties, which may arise on return to work and how best to deal with these situations. In the Cook Islands one of the major problems identified for some teachers was the perceived lack of support on return to school. One suggested the need for a follow-up 'pep course', whilst others suggested the need for a direct follow-up in the school by the trainer with direct contact with the teacher and the principal. As one teacher observed:

I feel there is a need for some sort of follow-up, either from the trainer or someone else who can pick up if a person hasn't quite got things right.

It was noted in Chapter 2 that a training curriculum that had clear objectives, was relevant to the work context and had varied content was important, as were, positive trainer characteristics, trainer credibility and performance feedback from the trainer. This was supported by comments from both Case Managers and teachers as is exemplified by the following comments:

I use the skills I learned every day, particularly empathy and negotiation skills. I'm proactive rather than reactive and therefore not in crisis mode all the time and the clients get quality service. I've learned to say 'no' and only make promises I can honour. I also feel more responsible to my work.

[We want a lecturer] ... 'full of life, snappy, understandable, easy to adjust, ... being alert ... easy going ... and one that can be positive. You're doing a good job of it so far. We want a lecturer like you.

The role of collaborative learning in facilitating transfer was discussed in Chapter 3. A teacher comment supports this:

I think if we need good relationships between participants, then there is no animosity, no feelings of distrust, no feelings of fear – I think you create a better atmosphere.

It was argued in Chapter 2 that for transfer to take place the nature of the training needs to be culturally appropriate and that it is not possible to simply transfer one form of training to different cultural contexts. One of the teachers in the Cook Islands study for example noted:

I think that whoever comes here has got to have a pretty good idea of what its like in our classrooms so they don't make assumptions about teaching that are not accurate. I think they have to have some ideas of what it is like to live here ... Like difficulties in actually living here ... by the time you get your planning done and cart your water from the creek and from the tank and community involvement.

Workplace characteristics

The workplace plays an important part in the transfer process, as it is here that the learner is expected to demonstrate their new knowledge and skills. If no change is perceived to have taken place, transfer is deemed not to have happened. Given this situation a number of studies have tried to establish what particular factors in the workplace facilitate transfer.

Direct supervisor support is seen as crucial, since the supervisor often determines whether new learning can be implemented at the workplace. This is highlighted by the following teacher and Case Manager comments:

I think the principal should be fully informed about the course and be given what the participants are to be given and the principal needs to be involved in pre-course meetings and things to make ... (him/her) ... more aware of what we are going to do and what we will be going through, so that they will be given more understanding of the course and they know what to expect.

If teachers are aware that the principal is supportive, they will do it well.

I think the principal needs to support them. Ask them – how did the course go? What did you learn today? Would you like to share it with other teachers here? [The principal should also] supply them with all the materials as required.

People at the branch were interested, as I could teach them stuff from the course. The Team Leader and PCM were supportive.

The branch climate has not let us do this – not to the extent we'd been encouraged to. On my return I tried to encourage staff to focus on getting out rather than processing, but it wasn't realistic. My approach is now more client focused and I try to impact this with other staff. There is little opportunity to change the organisation. Few resources to achieve things, because to change the organisation you need resources and abilities to do things.

In essence, the supervisor needs to be totally committed to the course or training programme, with their involvement being sought from the outset.

The importance of the socio-cultural factors of the work environment have been particularly emphasised by those writers who advocate for the training, or at least part of it, to take place in the workplace. This approach emphasises the importance of training being seen not merely as the acquisition of technical skills, but also as a social process. If the socialisation which takes place at training or on courses does not match that of the workplace environment, then there is potential for difficulties to arise. As one teacher stated:

> It is important that those who didn't attend the course say that you're doing it really good, [and they ask] ... can they have some time to come and see this approach that you are taking in the class ... we can then feel good about what we are doing when they tell people ... 'they are doing something for the benefit of the school, for the kids and the teacher'.

By having the training on-site, this disparity is less likely to occur, and for new employees in particular, the opportunity to become acquainted with the social processes of the work environment, as well as gaining new skills and knowledge, is provided.

The value of a supportive organisational culture and climate was highlighted by a Case Manager who stated that:

> When I returned from the course there was a very accepting environment in the branch and ACC to change – basically for the first year post course I was able to introduce a number of things, e.g. floating person to cover leave; discretion being legal; reducing case loads by half; support was there acknowledging skills and professionalism.

In addition, training programmes often provide a supportive environment for participants to work and develop in, an environment, which may not be replicated in the workplace – the 'widows and orphans effect'. One of the Cook Islands teachers commented about the frustrations of not being able to use the ideas:

> You go on this course and you come back and you're plonked totally in an environment where it can't be used. You're a keen teacher but you have to shut up.

Summary

The research and findings of the case studies presented in this book suggest that learner characteristics, course design and the work environment are crucial factors in facilitating transfer. Whilst all three factors are often viewed in isolation, Boud and Walker's model for promoting learning from experience (see Figure 1.1) incorporates all three. As indicated at the beginning of this chapter all of the elements were important in facilitating transfer in our research. The following chapter provides our reflection on the research in terms of the key factor that stood out for each of us with respect to learning about the transfer of learning. Despite the differences between the case studies, the interrelationships between the participant responses are also highlighted.

References

Boud, D. and Walker, D. (1990). *Studies in Continuing Education*, **12**, 61–80.
Bransford, J. D. and Schwartz, D. L. (1999). *Review of Research in Education*, **24**, 61–100.

8 *Modelling Transfer: Reflection on Action*

What meta-factors facilitated transfer in each of the case studies? This chapter is the researchers' reflection on their case study. Each researcher highlights the factor, which was most apparent for them when reflecting on transfer and their research. However, despite the differences in both the context and the courses, there are a number of commonalities between the three case studies. All of the participants were mature students, engaged in tertiary education course designed to promote their personal and professional development. There was a mix of age and gender, and all three courses facilitated preparation for future transfer.

Responses from participants, in all three studies, demonstrated the integration of the learning in their work and personal lives, the importance of support and feedback, and the recognition that change was ongoing. The importance of personal and professional development is exemplified with the Case Manager research, support by the Cook Islands teachers and preparation for future transfer by the Business Studies students.

At the end of this chapter the main conclusions for ensuring transfer of learning are summarised in key points.

Personal and professional development

The Diploma in Rehabilitation Studies aimed to develop participants both personally and professionally, rather than focusing exclusively on professional development as is often the case in workplace training. This was also the case in the other two studies. The elements of the course which focused on this included the Personal and Professional Development Day (Tuesday), the *noho marae* (sleeping in a Maori meeting house) and the Practicum (see Chapter 4 for more details). This mix was reported on favourably by the participants, as is shown by the following observations.

It was good, excellent – I would never have coped with full-on study. The combination of personal and professional worked well because the personal part is so important in the role of rehabilitation. You have to be a part of people's lives, but must also be able to stand back.

The practicum was a good confidence thing in getting it finished and over-coming obstacles – doing something a bit different, it really increased my confidence. The mixing of personal and professional was quite important and tied in well, particularly in terms of learning about the impact you have on others.

Tuesdays involved a lot of soul searching amongst yourself even though I didn't like it at the time it's made me see who I really am and what my strengths and weaknesses are. The marae environment was taken for granted by me but I realised this wasn't necessarily so for the next person. I now have a deeper appreciation of other people's interpretation of things – even life itself. I know better what people's comfort zones are and I now take people for who they are.

For me Tuesdays were most important because they made you look at yourself as a person. The marae was another example because you learned to centre yourself. I now know who I am – know my strengths and weaknesses and that unless I'm doing something I believe in I'm wasting my time.

The majority of the participants were women and for some this was the first time they had been away from home for an extended period of time. The exposure to new places and ideas meant that some of the women started to question the lives they were leading, probably influenced by the personal and professional day, where participants were encouraged to reflect on themselves and their lives through a variety of different activities. Also the *noho marae* had a strong influence on some participants as they were in an environment that encouraged them to search for their roots, where they stood and what was important to them in life. All of this was aimed at having Case Managers who knew themselves, were comfortable with where they were at, so that they were then able to deal with the diverse client needs presented to them on a daily basis.

Increased self-confidence in both home and work life, enabling me to make changes.

I have more personal worth or self-worth as I now realise that I can make a difference in other people's lives.

I feel I now have more empathy with clients and look at things from different angles. I also try to wipe out my personal issues before talking to clients so that I can focus on them. My personal growth from the course has affected my practice in terms of better interviewing and negotiating. The marae gave me more of a sense of trying to understand where clients are coming from. I've made changes in my practice and feel that it has been beneficial to the people, but not necessarily cost-efficient in terms of ACC.

Two women separated from their husbands during the course. The first one because her husband could not deal with the fact that his wife was getting a university qualification which he did not have. The other because she discovered that she really had little in common with her partner. Both went on to move up in the organisation professionally. Some women were still running their families whilst on the course. They would spend all week in Wellington then go home at the weekend to prepare the meals for the following week, as well as do the cleaning and washing and their assignments. For one of the men the realisation was that he had always undersold himself. The main change he made was to apply for a senior position in Head Office necessitating a move away from his provincial location where he had been born and lived ever since – a big risk for someone of his age and with a family to move as well. A similar story applied to a solo mother from the course who applied for a job at Head Office and moved from one of the smaller cities to Wellington – again with her increased self-confidence she was able to do this.

In my personal life there has been a willingness to take risks – we've done that as a family and it has paid off.

This issue of home and family responsibilities in the Cook Islands study was also particularly significant for a number of the participants, who were predominantly women.

The following comments were made by the ACC participants up to two years after they had completed the course and provide examples of transfer that combine the personal with the professional.

Personal development has been the key for me as I think a lot more about myself and how my make-up affects other people and also that there are lots of different ways of doing my job. I'm much more sensitive and professional in my approach now, whereas in the past I was too bureaucratic. I haven't been able to change as much as I would have liked to because there is a conflict of interest between insurance and rehabilitation ... I'd like to work really differently, so I'm trying to find a happy medium. There is an ongoing amount of change in ACC with a high level of staff turnover. (12 months)

I have had a huge turnover in files – having the third most closures in the branch. I've had a lot of people who have done courses and then found work. It's hard to say I apply a particular skill from the course, but it's given me the confidence to apply everything ... I'd take short cuts because it's a numbers game, not really rehabilitation ... I have far more confidence in what I'm doing the more I do it. What I now do is have far more face-to-face interviews, as people react so much differently ... Personal contact makes a huge difference and also provides better outcomes. (18 months)

I think the mere fact that I did succeed and achieve results gave me more confidence than I ever had ... For me I needed to learn about listening as I wasn't a very good listener. I was judged by my peers in the Threes Exercise, so now in meetings I ask myself am I really listening to them and do I hear what they are saying? I am now able to run meetings and workshops and have good negotiation skills. I think I have more of an awareness that other people have needs and things they want to say and even if I'm ten steps ahead of them I need to listen to them. (24 months)

The practicum was the key in bringing skills back to the work place because with the learning contract I set goals and for me the things I set out were my weaknesses, so it made me do it properly. Overall the course has had a lot of effect on how I work ... A lot of staff come to me to ask advice on IRPs [Individual Rehabilitation Plan] and vocational stuff and I know that those areas were very new to me when I started as a Case Manager. My IRPs are now tight enough so that if they go to review we win. I put that down to a lot of the skills we learned on the course, like analysing skills ... I've put into practice across the board what we learned on the course. They are now part of me and who I am – it comes naturally I don't have to think about it ... Prior to the course I didn't contribute as much. (24 months)

It was really beneficial to have gone through the course, as I've done more goal setting and striving to achieve them. It's given me more confidence in my personal and work environment. I haven't used everything from the course, like the legislation, but I have used the analysis, documentation, communication and interviewing skills ... I now have more confidence and am not frightened to raise points or speak my mind, before the course I was quite shy ... The course has made people stronger, as you tend not to develop your own skills because you are focusing on what ACC wants you to do. They underestimate you and don't let you strive and there is never any follow-up on courses throughout the organisation. (24 months)

The key learning from this case study includes:

- Being aware of the effect courses can have on participants personally as well as professionally;
- Sometimes transfer happens in unexpected domains;
- Ensuring that the course meets the requirements of both the organisation and individuals;
- Having safety nets in place;
- Having qualified staff to deal with potential issues unrelated to the course or a referral system.

This case study has highlighted the importance of personal and professional learning for facilitating transfer, also the notion of unintended or unexpected learning, and the role of the educator in providing support for learners. The other two studies would support these findings, but this factor was most apparent in the Case Manager research. The transfer in these situations provides a third alternative to the negative and positive transfer positions. In positive transfer the initial learning transfers to the new situation, in negative transfer the initial or prior learning interferes with new learning (for example, language learning). The third alternative is learning as a catalyst for personal transformation and change, where learning may lead to a re-evaluation of identity, values, and dispositions. Such learning leads to change.

Support

The findings, observations and experiences of the researcher in the Cook Islands study, resulted in a number of clearly identified strategies that maximised opportunities for teachers to transfer ideas from the course to the classroom (see Chapter 5 for more details). Although the research did not identify the relative impact of specific strategies, it became obvious that a range of inter-related approaches were contributing to transfer effectiveness.

The research in the Cook Islands identified that the 'before – during – after' model was very appropriate. There was significance given to the key stakeholders' roles during the differing time periods to enhance transfer of the training. One of the key criticisms of previous workshops and courses was that trainers had 'flown in and out' without adequate preparation and understanding of the context and did not engage in any follow-up activities. This research highlighted that a needs analysis prior to the course was vital, and that personal growth and links to lifestyle were an important component of the transfer process, as was the case in the ACC research. This understanding of the needs should be reflected in the course content and that teachers should be given the opportunity to demonstrate their newly developed skills and behaviours in the classroom.

> Before you actually launched this course you made sure you actually came here and actually observed teachers in a classroom ... because it is a different environment to your environment. You've got to come to know how they react to certain suggestions and things like that before you actually start thinking about what will be the content of the course.

During the course there has to be relevant activities. The teachers needs to feel it ... that they understand the things thoroughly ... they can then put it across to their children. They will use those ideas with them.

One of the things is to try the ideas in the school. But we need the time and the opportunity to do this.

Undoubtedly, the social support given and received from others was a significant means of motivating the teacher to participate in the course activities and accomplish a pass in the paper. Support as a means for impacting in the classroom is consistent with the international literature, but in the Cook Islands setting its value was markedly apparent. Being a society in which the individual and group are 'one' this is not surprising and it was a significant theme identified in the research. The support to and from others enhanced *aroha* and lessened opportunity for *akama*.

I think it is causing a desire for them to continue with it, to extend more, to develop further. If you are getting support, you feel like carrying on with it, you are enthusiastic about it and you keep on. If you run out of ideas you will be looking for other ideas whereas if you're not enthusiastic, you'll just do what you know then and let it drop.

I think it is just the security [for you] that somebody cares and [is] complimenting on what you are doing ... you know that your colleagues are proud of what you are doing.

The support was in various forms, but centred on the course participant sharing with others the ideas of the course, clarifying meaning and/or getting feedback from others about what they were doing. There were various means of accomplishing this, some more formal than others. In the Cook Islands and ACC research, family and community support, as well as recognition for the students' efforts was an important form of support and on a number of occasions family members were involved willingly in the opening, closing, and certification ceremonies. A number of teachers mentioned this:

Yes, that's also important. The support from ... my family at home ... they need to make sure they support me at this.

A lot of our teachers are women and their husbands don't want them doing anything extra – they think that time belongs to them, that time belongs to the family. They think that you do your school work at school and you finish it at school and you shouldn't be coming home and spending lots of time doing it, or giving up your holidays or whatever it is.

Informal networking amongst teachers (for example, helping one another with assignments and getting feedback from others) and formal tutorial meetings to consolidate the course learning were other means of support.

Actually we want them [non-participating staff members/colleagues/friends] to support us. If they don't want to join into the course we would like their support if we are to do something in the school ... because there are times when we need them, when we need to ask their opinions.

Ministry of Education acknowledgement and school management and principal encouragement and interest in the teacher's participation and accomplishments were additional means of support considered important by the teachers.

Teachers are not willing to go out of their way to improve their work in the classroom if the Ministry of Education staff are not giving their support.

The giving of support to others (for example, helping implement course ideas for non-course participants) by course members was also highly valued as a means of legitimising the course outcomes.

[An acknowledgment from the non-course participants that] ... you're doing it really good, [and they ask] ... can they have some time to come and see this approach that you are taking in the class ... [people can then] ... feel good about what they are doing when they tell people ... they are doing something for the benefit of the school, for the kids and the teacher.

Related to this notion of the importance of support were other considerations such as the nature and levels of support needed. For example, school enrolment patterns on the courses determined in many ways the intensity of the support that was provided. It was readily noticed that the teacher's pace of change related to the level of enrolment of the school staff and, in particular, whether senior professional management were course members. Teachers were able to network readily and seek support to observe and discuss ideas. Legitimacy of implementation of ideas was available. On the courses in which there were a number of participants from the same school then these became 'communities of learners' within the workshop. Group activities often became a competitive (yet friendly) activity between each school cluster, encouraging teachers to achieve at high levels. Hence the problems associated with off-campus courses were not apparent with many of the courses in which the majority of staff members were enrolled.

We like to work together in our school groups. I can help her and she can help me because we know the classrooms we come from. When we go back to school we have got something to talk about and we can help each other use the ideas.

After the course ... sharing between two buddies ... is excellent, I always ask her to come and observe me, and when she is working sometimes she gets stuck and asks me 'why do you do that?' Then I share with her all the activities on the course I've been doing. She understands. 'No buddy is no good'.

Who was giving the support and to whom the support was given were significant factors in determining the success of transfer. For example, if a support person was of higher status (for example principal, Ministry of Education official) then the support was more highly valued, but if the recipient of the support was more highly trained and experienced than the supporter then it was likely to have less impact.

I think the principal should be fully informed about the course and be given what the participants are to be given and the principal needs to be involved in pre-course meetings and things to make

... [him/her] ... more aware of what we are going to do and what we will be going through, so that they will be given more understanding of the course and they know what to expect.

When the support was given was also of importance – it was recognised that initial support helped to motivate the teachers to participate, support during the course maintained the momentum and encouraged completion of assignments, whilst follow-up support was considered to be particularly valuable for continued implementation of ideas.

Underlying this support to and from others was the key idea of maintaining favourable relationships and the value that had for assisting with the implementation of ideas.

I think if we have good relationships between participants, then there is no animosity, no feelings of distrust, no feelings of fear – I think you create a better atmosphere. We want teachers who want to get ... involved and share ideas.

If there was no support evident or there was wariness by others for the teacher's implementation of ideas, then relationship problems could readily arise.

There is often a lack of support within the environment, within the teaching environment. There's almost jealousy – not, not really jealousy, but there is a pull-you-down [attitude] which actually means putting it into place is not that easy. It's not as easy as the tutor thinks it is. [Some teachers will say]. 'Oh, that's not new, we've been doing that for years ... you think that is going to work? I've been teaching for years, I know better than that.'

I know islanders. Somebody goes up we tend to pull them down. We tend to go and gossip ... and that puts you down. Sometimes you have this feeling why am I doing it? Just one single mistake you make and they jump on you and that is the fear of most teachers over here. Just to make a mistake and then everybody pull you down or criticise you. That's what it is, and that's why they need support ... Over here it's a big black mark [if you make a mistake] ... and over here you can't reason with some teachers. 'I'm right and that's it. Final!' There are no other options.

Related to the importance of social support were the trainer's characteristics. It was evident that a trainer, who enjoyed interacting with the participants, who planned carefully for the local context, who understood the local context and was 'in' the community was considered to be a key factor in developing a programme that was likely to be more relevant and hence course ideas were more likely to have sustainability. The trainer who understood the culture of the environment (organisational and national) was regarded more highly as a teacher, because he had a background of understanding for the development and delivery of the course programme in context.

You have also got to think of the charisma of the coordinator. I think that is important. You get someone up here doing a course who is boring, it can turn you right off. You need someone who is praising and encouraging.

I think that whoever comes here has got to have a pretty good idea of what its like in our classrooms so they don't make assumptions about teaching that are not accurate. I think they have to have some ideas of what it is like to live here. Like difficulties in actually living here ...

by the time you get your planning done and cart your water from the creek and from the tank and community involvement.

Training content that was practical, relevant, locally-referenced and useful to others in the school was important to the course participants. Particular significance was given to course methodology that ensured active and collaborative approaches to learning. Interestingly course notes (summaries of the day's activities) were also regarded very highly, as these became a series of *aide memoire* and assisted the teacher to implement ideas at a later date. This was similar to the learning journals kept by both the ACC Case Managers and the business students.

The activities need to be fun, we need to laugh and we need to work together on the assignments. Sometimes we like to play games and beat the other team.

These notes that you give us are important for planning. And the principal wants to see them too!

The above discussion has highlighted what the author perceived to be the key factors relating to transfer success. One of the key determinants, support, was recognised as particularly important in the transfer literature; in this context it was considered to be vital if the teachers were to implement and sustain changes in the classroom. Indeed, most of the other factors (for example, trainer qualities, programme characteristics, programme–culture match) can be interpreted as logistical support factors as well. The key message for trainers working in any environment, is that for training to be effective there needs to be more than a fleeting acknowledgement of the local cultural context. This factor was also important in the context of the ACC organisational culture and the culture of being a distance student with the Open Polytechnic.

Preparation for future transfer

The Bachelor of Business degree in the case study was designed to be practical and course development teams were encouraged to build assignments and assessments around workplace applications and examples. The overall philosophy of the degree emphasised the development of generic skills such as communication, technology and critical thinking. It highlighted the importance of preparation for future transfer, with particular reference to the transfer process, the instructional approaches used, learning experiences which facilitated transfer and application to different settings (see Chapter 6 for more details).

Publicity material for prospective students referred to the need for employees to be self-motivated and accomplished problem solvers. The Bachelor of Business 2000 Programme Guide stated: 'the principle aim of the Bachelor of Business programme is to promote skills, competencies and attributes which are valued by the wider business community. The Bachelor of Business focuses on developing skills in effective thinking, communication and relationship building' (Open Polytechnic of New Zealand, 2000, p.6).

The participants in the case-study provided many and diverse examples of transfer of learning. Over the years of their degree studies the participants learned or developed generic skills such as self-management (time-management, self-confidence, planning and determination), communication and thinking skills. In addition the students developed their skills as 'learners', and their awareness of learning as a deliberate process.

The work across a number of courses in the degree required repeated adaptation and application of generic skills. Initially, skills such as time-management and planning may have been formally introduced within one course, but with repeated use became habits which were automatically utilised within other courses. The other two case studies had similar findings. The evidence from the business studies case study was that multiple and diverse applications enhanced fluency and automaticity in a range of skills including self-management, problem-solving, report-writing and financial skills. Applying skills and knowledge in workplace settings and within changing work roles also reinforced the likelihood of transfer.

> You're fumbling at the beginning of the course to do something like that, and at the end you're just racing through it. So, as your confidence built up, it took the same amount of time to do an assignment that was worth perhaps forty percent as it did to the first assignment, which may have been worth ten percent. Because you just had that confidence. ... What I think it was trying to do was to focus on perhaps the most important thing for our organisation, what we needed to know mostly, and by doing a course on SWOT analysis and these various other phases three or four times, you sort of – it became ingrained by the end of the course, as to how to approach this, how to actually think strategically, I guess.

The fact that most of the business students were employed and had opportunities to apply their learning within the context of their employment, provided a context for future transfer to occur. In other words, the students had the will or disposition and the means to transfer their learning to workplace situations.

> I try any course I've done, I look at how I can adapt that into the workplace, so then I'm going to get some experience from the course at work. So I guess I'm trying to make the course work for me.

Some students lacked opportunities to apply learning within their current workplace contexts, as with the Case Managers and Cook Islands teachers. The 'spirit of transfer' makes a difference in these situations. One student, while finding his management course relevant to his current job also thought about how he could apply what he was learning to his plans to run his own company in the future.

The disposition, or perhaps more rightly the dispositions, involved in transfer can be nurtured within instructional programmes. Here we are talking about the dispositions of being open-minded, curious, confident, persistent, being an ongoing learner, and willing to seek help. The experiences of the business students provided evidence that dispositions as 'attitudes' or 'habits' were nurtured during the degree and were transferable to workplace and other situations. Encouraging learners to think about:

- Potential opportunities to apply learning;
- Applying learning in the diverse settings;
- Discussing what they have been learning with colleagues;
- Identifying barriers to workplace applications;
- Identifying what resources exist to support transfer of learning;
- Making connections between current learning and previous experiences; and
- Identifying what might be done differently another time.

The business studies research focused on what instructional approaches appear to make a difference in terms of future transfer of learning. In the case study attention was paid to examples of transfer and to the original learning. Two factors which facilitate future transfer and are applicable to all three case studies are:

1. Building on what a learner brings to the course (experiences, motivations, and goals); and
2. Emphasis on real workplace problems.

Learners need to be encouraged to think of their learning in terms of future transfer, rather than as preparation for an examination or essay. The business studies research supported the argument of cognitive theorists on the pivotal role that the encoding and organisation of knowledge plays, in the accessibility and retrieval of that knowledge in new and different situations.

The findings highlighted the importance of linking learning to real workplace problems and situations, as was the case in the ACC and Cook Islands research. When learners applied what they were learning to real problems and situations, they appeared to engage in deep, rather than surface learning, by:

- Providing multiple and diverse examples;
- Linking theory to practice;
- Using problem-solving approaches;
- Using authentic problems from learner's work or social context;
- Modelling the type of questions that would facilitate the transfer of learning;
- Encouraging reflective practice through the use of journals or similar, and the inclusion of tasks requiring learners to notice and to interpret features of transfer contexts; and
- Building self-assessment exercises into courses.

As one of the business studies participant's stated:

Because in terms of one of the assessments, you do actually have to do practical things rather than theory. Even the management paper I did, I had to interview my boss around a set questionnaire that was in there. So it's not all make believe. You actually have to take all this theory, interview your boss, and then analyse the results.

The participants did not necessarily appreciate the value of what they later came to see as effective instructional approaches. In a number of courses students were required to keep a learning journal, and some started out finding this irksome.

But by the time you are onto your fifth journal, you get the hang of what they were doing it. … I felt good because you could actually put down your thoughts in writing, whereas before you'd just think about it. And it makes a difference to actually think about something and put it down on paper. Then you can always look back on it as well. Whereas if you had a thought and hadn't written it down, it's gone.

The use of real workplace problems helps students become comfortable with questioning, discussing and reflecting on workplace problems. In many cases they also identify support and resources within their working environment.

Well, one reason, of course, is the structured, formal reason that I'm doing one of assignments or a part of the project I'm working through, that I'm asking for help with, or interviewing somebody about. The other thing is points of interest. I've read something or covered something which applies entirely to a situation or a person I see managing in a role.

The case study of transfer of learning within the context of the business degree highlighted the value of preparation for future transfer. The students benefited from the interaction of work-based learning experiences with course-based learning, as in the other case studies. From an educational practitioner's viewpoint the key learning points were:

- The depth and breadth of learning transfer was enhanced by multiple, diverse and applied learning experiences, and
- Instructional design.

Conclusions

This book has emphasised the importance of matching the programme or course of study to the requirements of the participants and therefore the need to design a custom made curriculum for each situation. It is rarely possible to simply develop a programme or course and implement it in a different context with different learners. In order to match programme and student needs, the course designer must have a very clear understanding of the transfer process and transfer principles highlighted in this book. A key factor in this, is understanding the participants' requirements from their perspective, an area previously underrepresented in the literature. Much of the previous research on transfer has been from a course designer or organisational perspective, with the voice of participants often restricted to short evaluation sheets on completion of the learning experience.

Through the theory and practice highlighted in this book, we have shown how the participants in three very different learning contexts feel about transfer and the factors that have facilitated their learning. In general, the case studies in this book support the theoretical concepts underpinning the transfer of learning and in particular Boud and Walker's (1990) model of promoting learning from experience as discussed in Chapter 1.

The main conclusions with respect to facilitating the transfer of learning to be drawn from the research presented are:

- Transfer is a multi-dimensional process and is mediated by the characteristics of the individual (for example, motivation, attitudes, expectations and behaviours), the learning/training programme (for example, the nature of the activities) and the social/cultural contexts (for example, the level of support and co-operative vs competitive values). A learning/training programme, therefore, needs to incorporate a strategic and integrated approach to learning and ensure that each of these domains receives adequate consideration in planning.
- Transfer is related to what occurs before the specific learning/training event(s), what occurs during the specific learning/training programme and what occurs after the learning/training. Educators and trainers, therefore, need to view learning/training as a process not an outcome that simply arises from a learning/training programme. It is a complex process that involves a number of key stakeholders and events.

- Transfer is intimately related to other key learning/training dimensions – for example, adult learning principles, change in organisations and professional development approaches impact significantly on the job. The educator needs to understand these connections and utilise them in planning for transfer.
- A key determinant of training programmes is the need to support trainees to use the new skills and behaviours on-the-job. It is insufficient to deliver a course and expect transfer to occur to the workplace. The setting of goals/tasks, the application of these and monitoring of performance is useful within a social context.
- By combining personal and professional development in course design and delivery the potential for transfer of learning to be realised is enhanced. This is particularly important with adult learners whose personal and professional lives tend to be inextricably linked.
- An analysis of the work environment is important to identify the level and types of support available, the barriers to transfer, the opportunities for transfer, the level of similarity between the new behaviour and existing behaviours, the climate for change and the consequences of change.
- Because transfer is a process, simple outcome measures are insufficient to determine the level of transfer. Often there will be a gap between what has been learned and application of learning to another setting. This is particularly common where behavioural change has taken place such as in the development of communication skills. Applying learning that is more generic may take longer to transfer than specific task-related skills, such as using a new software package that is required in daily practice.
- The research presented in this book indicated that transfer can occur, but that it needs to be planned for and transfer strategies strategically implemented. From a participant's perspective this is particularly important in terms of course design and post-course follow-up. This ensures preparation for future transfer.
- There are a range of strategies, understandings and approaches that facilitate transfer. Educators and trainers need to be fully aware of these in order to select the appropriate approach for the context within which they are working, to maximise the chances of transfer. The technology of transfer needs to be an important part of the facilitator's repertoire of skills.
- Transfer involves team and collaborative skills and is best considered in terms of a social context.

Summary

Underpinning this chapter is the intention of highlighting the meta-factors that facilitate transfer. To assist with the process, the researchers each needed to reflect on and extract what they, as practitioners, had learnt from course participants about facilitating transfer. The three factors identified create conditions for developing knowledge, behaviours and attitudes that may be adaptable to new and different situations. Readers will relate to the three factors based on their unique set of prior experiences, motivations and theories about teaching and learning. The conclusions arising from the study provide a framework for ensuring an effective process of transfer occurs in a variety of contexts.

Epilogue

This book has provided participant perspectives of adult education and training in the context of the transfer of learning. We have argued that the foundation of the transfer of learning is the ability to promote learning from experience, as highlighted in the Boud and Walker model introduced in Chapter 1 and referred to throughout the book.

The process of writing this book has been a transfer experience for us. We have brought our previous knowledge and experience together, synthesised these and applied our new perspectives to writing this book. Undoubtedly, this will impact upon our future endeavours in facilitating transfer – and we hope it will assist you too.

Reference

Boud, D. and Walker, D. (1990). *Studies in Continuing Education*, **12**, 61–80.
Open Polytechnic of New Zealand (2000). *Bachelor of Business Programme Guide*. Open Polytechnic of New Zealand, Wellington, New Zealand.

Further Research

There is still a need for further research in the area of transfer, particularly in terms of participant perspectives and the testing of the models described in Chapters 4–6 of this book. The following areas have been identified as options for future research.

With regard to the Case Manager study, conducting a two-year longitudinal qualitative study had its challenges in terms of keeping in touch with participants, particularly when they moved jobs and the organisation was restructured twice during the research period. A number of areas for future research are highlighted:

- *The proposed transfer of learning model should be tested in other human service organisations.* The perceived positive relationships between key themes, in particular, need to be considered in different situations to determine their influences on the transfer of learning. The phenomenological approach adopted for this research has considered the experiences of a particular group of people over time. This provided a number of insights into the transfer of learning from the classroom to the workplace. The more positivistic psychological study undertaken by Collinson and Brook (1997) examined similar issues with a larger sample of the same population, but came to similar conclusions. The combined outcomes from these two pieces of research indicate that there is merit in testing the proposed transfer of learning model in other situations to enhance its validity and applicability to the human services in wider terms.
- *The link between the transfer of learning and service management should be investigated in other settings.* This research suggests that the transfer of training/learning should be regarded as an integral component of an organisation's service management strategy. In order for this to eventuate it is necessary for the organisation to take a holistic approach to educational programmes. Consultation, communication and commitment, throughout the organisation, are vital for this approach to be successful. The challenge here is for government organisations, which often have little or no control over significant changes that are imposed on them.
- *The impact of setting and duration of training on the transfer of learning should be considered more closely.* The combination of on- and off-site training appears to have been important in facilitating the transfer of learning for participants involved in this research. There was, however, little evidence to suggest whether the duration of the programme was significant or not. These factors are particularly important as they have direct financial implications for organisations considering training opportunities. Research identifying the impact of setting and duration would be particularly valuable if it was linked with the type of learning outcome desired by the organisation that is specific task development, personal development or a combination of the two.
- *More research should be conducted which focuses on the experiences of training participants.* Most of the research on the transfer of learning has been based on the perceptions of training providers and workplace supervisors or managers. This research is one of few

studies which has considered the impact of training on participants. There also appears to be a limited amount of research examining the long-term impact of participation in adult learning opportunities, which link people with their working lives – recommendation also made by Benseman (1996). More research in the area of participants' experiences will assist in providing a more complete picture of the transfer of learning process. This will be particularly valuable if this is in the form of long-term longitudinal studies, as the majority of research on the transfer of learning only considers the period six months post-training. Organisations, however, are increasingly interested in the long-term benefits they will derive from investing in training and development programmes.

This research undertaken in the Cook Islands highlighted a number of significant factors that are important for implementation and theoretical development of transfer of training. The model and identification of strategies can be applied to decision-making and action in many training situations. Given that this research was designed to provide some answers to what constitutes effective transfer of training in a cultural context, it has also given prominence to a range of issues that further research needs to investigate. The following issues are suggested as directions for additional research:

- *The findings of this research project need to be subject to additional investigation.* For example, the value of support in other training contexts and with different samples. Would the findings from the present study apply to other professional/non-professional groups? What impact does base training outside this research setting have upon the need for social support? For those who have returned to the Cook Islands, what impact does living in a Western society have upon the level of support considered desirable?
- *Further examination of the nature of support and its bearing upon change processes is warranted.* What levels of support are needed? In what situations is support detrimental to transfer of training? What is the relationship of change to transfer in different cultural settings?
- *There is scope for further examining the role of specific strategies in transfer but also being mindful of the interactive nature of many of the variables.* For example, are there identifiable personality variables in the Cook Islands setting that promote change processes more readily? What factors make an individual more resilient/susceptible to negative feedback? Are changes to a system more readily accepted if introduced by an outsider to the system? What are the specific qualities that are needed for a principal to become a change agent in a system that is resistant to change?
- *What learning processes occur (and need to occur) when trainers develop expertise to work in cross-cultural settings with emphasis upon ensuring transfer?* How can trainers best prepare themselves to work in different cultural settings? How can this be best accomplished?
- *In a society that has a traditional conservatism and an emphasis upon certainty, what is the best means of creating within this system the notion of continuous inquiry and a community of learners to ensure transfer occurs?* How can needed change occur more readily in school systems and in teacher knowledge and skill? What impact does this have upon the culture?
- *Can the frameworks that have been developed by this research be used not only for planning but also as diagnostic tools to remediate difficulties in training programmes?* How many strategies and what combination of strategies best meet situations to ensure that a course is likely to succeed?
- *Lessons can be learnt from examining failures in transfer. In this research setting there are many reported anecdotal instances when this has occurred. This provides an excellent opportunity to further develop understanding of transfer of training.* What are the factors identified that

contribute to the transfer failure? What are the different perspectives on this failure? Can it be predicted?

- *Differing theoretical perspectives can contribute to these findings. Investigations of the research findings could be expanded upon if other perspectives are considered.* For example, in the domain of psychological inquiry, need theory, motivational perspectives and social cognitive approaches to explaining behaviour could expand upon how support contributes to an individual's psyche. Sociological inquiry could investigate the functional elements of support and its force as a moderating and innovating element in society.

The research on distance learning degree identified that using both qualitative and quantitative methodologies was an extremely effective approach for meeting the objectives of the research. It is an approach that would be worthwhile using again for similar studies. The current study, while making a significant contribution to the literature on transfer of learning also raised a number of questions which merit further research. The following are recommendations for future research on transfer of learning:

- *A longitudinal study of a cohort* that would begin when they first enrolled for the degree and would follow them over the years of the degree study exploring the influence of various factors on initial learning, and transfer. This would facilitate understanding of the mechanisms of transfer and how they are refined over time.
- *A study which included measures such as reports from colleagues, managers and clients.* The current research of necessity relied on self-reporting as the measure of transfer. It is acknowledged that within a distance education context there would be considerable logistical challenges to setting up a project which included more 'objective' measures of transfer. However, the importance of transfer to education merits such attention.
- *A longitudinal study of the development of transfer appropriate dispositions.* The current study highlighted the role dispositions play in transfer, and suggested that dispositions are nurtured within the learning experience and transfer to new and different situations. It would be valuable to gain a picture of what is required to foster the development of transfer appropriate dispositions, and how learners actively utilise such dispositions in transfer situations.
- *A study of learners enrolling in a different vocationally oriented degree qualification (teaching, nursing, library studies).* Would such a study yield similar results?
- *A study of learners enrolling in a trades qualification offered by distance.* Would a study of learners enrolling in a trades qualification offered by distance yield similar results?
- *A comparative study of mature learners engaged in part-time study for a business degree in a contact institution.* This would assist in determining the extent to which distance learning facilitates the integration of learning and living, and to what extent the integration of learning and living is a characteristic of part-time study.
- *A meta-level research project of research studies of transfer of learning with the objective of developing a typology of transfer.* Can a typology of transfer be developed which identifies teaching/learning approaches which support particular types of transfer?
- *A study of transfer of learning from a course design perspective.* One of the gaps in the current study was the lack of data generated in relation to how transfer was addressed within instructional design. At no stage was it intended to conduct a detailed analysis of the content, structures and underpinning instructional design features of the course materials in relation to transfer of learning. Such a study would be worthwhile in the future. A future

study could commence during the course development phase and follow a course through its respective stages. This could involve a participant–observation role in relation to:

- design of the curriculum;
- identification of learning outcomes;
- underlying philosophy;
- choice of teaching, learning and assessment strategies;
- consultation (why, who, what, how, when);
- debates; and
- evaluation (what is evaluated, and who is involved in the evaluation process).

As can be seen from this Appendix, research in the area of transfer of learning is wide ranging and there is potential for further investigation in many aspects of the transfer process. The issues raised here are a starting point and by no means should be regarded as an exhaustive list.

References

Benseman, J. (1996) In *The Fourth Sector: Adult and Community Education in Aotearoa/New Zealand*. (eds, Benseman, J., Findsen, B. and Scott, M.) Dunmore Press Limited, Palmerston North, pp. 234–46.

Collinson, C. and Brook, J. (1997). *Transfer of Training: An Evaluation of Transfer from the Tertiary Setting to the Corporate Environment*. Massey University, Department of Psychology, Palmerston North, New Zealand.

Index